WORLD WONDERS

Published by Collins
An imprint of HarperCollins Publishers
Westerhill Road
Bishopbriggs
Glasgow G64 2QT
www.harpercollins.co.uk

A catalogue record for this book is available from the
British Library.

ISBN   978-0-00-836011-5

10 9 8 7 6 5 4 3 2 1

Printed in Slovenia

If you would like to comment on any aspect of this
book, please contact us at the above address or
online.
email: collins.reference@harpercollins.co.uk

f   facebook.com/collinsref

🐦 @collins_ref

WORLD WONDERS

Michał Gaszyński

discover the secrets of our planet's iconic structures

CONTENTS

WONDER LOCATIONS

Svalbard Global Seed Vault

Palace of Westminster & Westminster Abbey

Amsterdam Old Town

Berlin Wall

NORTH AMERICA

Stonehenge

Malbork Castle

Moscow Kremli

CN Tower

Habitat 67

Arc de Triomphe

Eiffel Tower

EUROPE

Leaning Tower of Pisa

Golden Gate Bridge

Central Park

Louvre

Statue of Liberty

Colosseum

World Trade Center & One World Trade Center

Guggenheim Museum Bilbao

Vatican City

Camp Nou

Acropolis of Athens

White House

Old City (Jerusale

Kennedy Space Center

Pentagon

Ouarzazate Solar Power Station

Petra

Du & Kh

Chichén Itzá

Bibliotheca Alexandrina

Great Mosque of Mecca

Great Mosque of Djenné

Suez Canal

Great Pyramids of Giza

AFRICA

SOUTH AMERICA

Machu Picchu

Brasília

Rio de Janeiro

Moai

WONDER CLASSIFICATION

∎ Architectural ∎ Cultural ∎ Historical ∎ Technological

Trans-Siberian Railway

SIA

Forbidden
City

Great Wall
of China

Three Gorges
Dam

Taj Mahal

Taipei 101

Angkor Wat

Petronas
Towers

Rabbit-Proof &
Dingo Fences

OCEANIA

Sydney Opera House

INTRODUCTION

Humans have been creating wondrous structures for millennia. The tools of our ancestors may have been more rudimentary than the technology we take for granted today, but their dreams and ambitions were just as extraordinary as our own. With teamwork, organisation and ingenuity, ancient humans were able to realise some incredible visions, from the humbling vastness of the Egyptian pyramids to the mystery of the carved moai of Easter Island, the intricate spectacle of the Colosseum and the supreme artistic harmony of the Parthenon.

As the centuries progressed, so too did the scope of what was possible. Buildings became bigger, taller and were made from remarkable new materials. Steel allowed skyscrapers such as the World Trade Center to stretch into the clouds. Concrete and advanced turbine technology enabled the building of the Three Gorges Dam, the biggest power station on the planet.

Some of the most spectacular structures were built to honour the gods, such as St Peter's Basilica, the Great Mosque of Mecca and Angkor Wat. Their scale and artistry aimed to transcend the mere mortal.

Many structures, like the Eiffel Tower, the Statue of Liberty and the Houses of Parliament, have become so iconic as landmarks that they are used to symbolise a whole nation. Others are amazing for their immense practicality: the Suez Canal revolutionised world trade and transportation.

A few of the most famous wonders were created simply to be beautiful. The Taj Mahal is a monument to lost love. In Paris, a medieval fortress was transformed into the largest art gallery in the world: the Louvre. The unmistakable Sydney Opera House was built as a fitting home to the finest music and drama.

In recent decades we have even left the surface of our planet, travelling into the heavens to build the incredible International Space Station.

In this wonderful book, Michał Gaszyński presents a selection of the most spectacular World Wonders in his own unique visual style. The images beautifully capture the majesty of the wonders, and the accompanying facts will surprise and delight you.

One thing is certain: we as humans will not stop creating wonderful things. Who knows what we will achieve in the years yet to come? Until that future is realised we hope you will enjoy this book as a record of human ingenuity, imagination and of dreams made real.

Welcome to World Wonders.

The Statue of Liberty was constructed by Gustave Eiffel, creator of the Eiffel Tower in Paris.

HABITAT 67

Montreal, Canada
Construction: 2 years (1964–1966)

The inspired creativity of Habitat 67 has made it one of the most recognisable and spectacular buildings in Montreal and Canada. This modernist landmark was designed as a model community that would significantly improve the lives of urban city-dwellers.

It was conceived by then-master's student Moshe Safdie, and was built as a pavilion for the World's Fair held in Montreal in 1967.

Design

Built in a brutalist architectural style, the project aimed to add the benefits of suburban living, such as gardens, privacy and fresh air, to a modern urban apartment building.

Architect

Moshe Safdie, an Israeli-Canadian architect, designed Habitat 67 at the age of just 29 as his graduate thesis. Another of his famous designs is the Marina Bay Sands Hotel in Singapore, known for its spectacular infinity pool 191 m (627 ft) above the ground.

Visionary failure

Habitat 67 is recognised as an architectural wonder, but it failed to have the revolutionary effect on the affordable housing market that its architect envisioned.

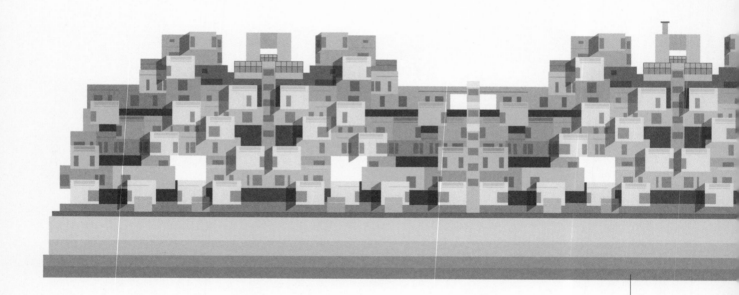

Expo 67

Habitat 67 was built for Expo 67, the most successful World's Fair of the 20th century. Today it is one of only two pavilions built for the fair that still stand.

Expo's 67 theme was 'Man and His World'. It hosted displays from 62 countries and had 50.3 million visitors, including the highest-ever World's Fair single day attendance of 569,500 visitors. The Montreal Metro was also constructed for this exhibition.

Location

The building stands in the harbour area by the St Lawrence River, giving residents a beautiful view of the estuary.

St Lawrence River

The river drains the basin of the Great Lakes into the Atlantic Ocean. Its estuary is the largest in the world.

Inspiration
The design was inspired by medieval towns that spread over hilltops in Mediterranean and Middle Eastern countries.

Modules
The building consists of 354 identical prefabricated concrete modules. Each apartment is made up of 1–8 modules and they are connected in different combinations to create a variety of living spaces.

Apartments
Originally there were 158 flats with areas ranging from 56–167 m². Some apartments were combined and there are now 146 homes. The masterplan was for the building to be expanded to have 1,200 apartments.

Terraces
Each flat has its own terrace located on the roof of neighbouring modules.

Lego
The first architectural models of the building were made with Lego bricks. The company plans to release a limited edition Habitat 67 Lego Architecture set.

Green surroundings
The area around the building is rich in plants and trees, contrasting pleasantly with the concrete of the structure.

Monument
In 2009, Quebec's Ministry of Culture classified Habitat 67 as a historic building.

CN TOWER

Toronto, Canada

Construction: 3 years (1973–1976)

When completed in 1976, the CN Tower was the tallest freestanding structure in the world. It still dominates Toronto's skyline and is a famous Canadian landmark. It offers spectacular views of Canada's largest city and Lake Ontario, the 13th largest lake by area in the world. Its height is also of practical use to the 16 national television, radio and other telecommunications providers that use it to transmit their signals.

"CN"
The initials stand for Canadian National, Canada's largest railway, which built the tower on a disused freight yard.

553.33 m
(1,815 ft)

Stand up straight
The CN Tower was built with incredible precision – from base to tip it is 2.79 cm (1.1 in) within plumb or true vertical.

A clear signal
The new skyscrapers being built in Toronto during the 1960s played havoc with radio and TV signals. Broadcasters needed a central antenna of at least 300 m, and so the idea for the CN tower was born.

Lightning
Every year, on average, 75 lightning strikes hit the top of the tower.

Visibility
When the conditions are good, from the top of the tower you can see places 160 km away, including Niagara Falls.

Antenna
Its 44 pieces were placed on top of the tower by a giant helicopter.

EdgeWalk
This amusement allows tourists attached to a harness to walk around the roof of the tower, lean out and hang 356 m above the ground.

The 360 Restaurant
It takes 72 minutes for this rotating restaurant to make one full revolution. It is located at 351 m.

Glass floor
Opened in 1995, it was the first of its kind in the world. It may look like a terrifying 342 m drop to the ground below, but its glass panels could bear the weight of 14 hippos (although they probably wouldn't fit in the lifts).

Modern Wonder of the World

In 1995, the American Society of Civil Engineers named the CN Tower as one of their Seven Modern Wonders.

The tallest

Although still the tallest structure in the Western Hemisphere, and the ninth-tallest overall, its record of tallest freestanding structure in the world was surpassed by the Burj Khalifa in 2007.

Top for dancing

The tower originally featured the highest disco in the world – Sparkles – on its indoor observation level.

Wind resistant

The tower was designed to stand strong in wind speeds of up to 418 km/h (260 mph).

Tourists

Every year, the tower is visited by over 1.5 million people.

Birds

During peak migration periods, the tower's lights are dimmed to prevent birds crashing into it.

Elevators

The tower is served by six elevators, which take 58 seconds to reach the top.

Concrete shaft

Its hexagonal shape provides stability and flexibility.

Earthquake resistant

The tower was built to withstand earthquakes up to 8.5 on the Richter scale.

335 m (1,100 ft)

CHICHÉN ITZÁ

Yucatán, Mexico
Construction: 8th–9th centuries

This pre-Columbian city is one of the most celebrated centres of the Mayan civilisation. Nestling amid a rambling jungle, it features precision-built pyramids, artistic temples and geometrically laid-out walkways. The flourishing culture that built Chichén Itzá had a mastery of many architectural styles that they exercised over several centuries.

In 1988, UNESCO recognised the archaeological importance of Chichén Itzá and included the site on its World Heritage List.

Ancient metropolis
Chichén Itzá is one of the largest cities built by the Maya people. Its buildings are spread over an area of 5 square kilometres (1.9 sq mi).

New wonder
In 2007, the city was named one of the New Seven Wonders of the World in an international poll.

"Cenote"
The city stands on a vast limestone plain that has no rivers or lakes but is dotted with natural sinkholes (cenotes) that provide plentiful water.

Sacred Cenote
Pre-Columbian Maya sacrificed objects and human beings into this cenote to worship the Mayan rain god, Chaac. It is 60 m (200 ft) in diameter and surrounded by sheer cliffs 27 metres (89 ft) high.

Etymology
Chichén Itzá in Mayan language means 'at the mouth of the well of the Itzá'.

Ceremonial Walkway

Great Ball Court
The ball court was used for playing an ancient Mesoamerican ballgame. No one knows the exact rules of this pastime, but it may have been similar to squash.

Temple of the Warriors
It has many similarities to buildings in Tula, over 1,000 km away, which indicates strong cultural connections between these regions.

EL CASTILLO

Osario
Similar to El Castillo but a little smaller, this pyramid has an opening on top that leads to a natural cave.

Chacmool
On top of the Temple of the Warriors is the Chacmool – a characteristic pre-Columbian Mesoamerican sculpture reclining on its elbows.

Group of a Thousand Columns

Market

Local power
The city was a major centre of power in the Northern Maya region.

Sound effects
The city is known for its mysterious sound effects. Clapping your hands creates multiple echoes that sound like bird calls.

Xtoloc Cenote
Well of sacrifice

El Caracol
This unique structure is over 1,000 years old and probably served as an astronomical observatory. Its name comes from the tower's spiral staircase – 'El Caracol' means snail in Spanish.

Tourists
With around 3 million visitors in 2017, Chichén Itzá is the second-most visited tourist site in Mexico, after Teotihuacan.

Population
The city had an estimated population of 50,000 people.

European discovery
The site was discovered by Spanish conquistadors in 1534. At first they met with no resistance from the Maya, but after couple of months the Spanish were forced out of the Yucatán Peninsula.

Advanced architecture
The city probably had a diverse population, which contributed to the rich variety of architecture.

EL CASTILLO
This iconic step-pyramid lies at the heart of the city complex. It is one of the most famous and popular pre-Columbian structures in Mexico.

Temple, not castle
The Spanish conquistadors assumed the building was a fortification and called it 'the castle'. But it was really a temple to the feathered serpent god Kukulkan.

All-powerful God
The construction on top of the pyramid was a temple to honour Kukulcan, the all-powerful feathered serpent god. Inside, priests performed rituals in his honour.

Jaguar throne
Archaeological excavations in the 1930s uncovered two hidden rooms inside the pyramid. Inside one was a jaguar-shaped throne, painted red using very rare cinnabar.

Shadow serpent
During the spring and autumn equinoxes, the sun casts a shadow along the corner edge of the pyramid's staircase creating the visual effect of a serpent crawling down the structure.

Panels
There are exactly 52 panels on each side of the pyramid. These represent the 52-year cycle of the Maya 'Calendar Round'.

Height
The pyramid structure is 24 m (79 ft) high with the temple adding another 6 m (20 ft) on top. The square base is 55 m (181 ft) on each side.

Pyramid over pyramid
Excavations in the 1930s discovered that El Castillo was built over a much older temple, probably also a pyramid.

365 steps
El Castillo has a total of 365 steps – one for every day of the year. There are 91 on each side and one on top that leads into the temple.

Mica
The inside walls of some of the buildings are lined with mica for insulation. This may have been brought from Brazil, thousands of kilometres away, which is incredible as the Maya probably did not have the wheel.

Acoustic effect
If you stand at the foot of the pyramid's north side and clap your hands, the echo sounds like a bird tweeting.

CENTRAL PARK

New York City, USA

Construction: 15 years (1857–1873)

Between 1821 and 1853, New York's population quadrupled. As the city expanded north up Manhattan island, the city authorities decided to create a large park on what was then a mostly uninhabited rocky, swampy landscape. Today, Central Park is an oasis of greenery in the heart of the city where people come to relax, exercise, soak up some culture or marvel at the spellbinding views. The park is the world's most-filmed location and one of the most recognisable symbols of the city.

Visitors
The park is visited by 42 million people every year, equivalent to the population of Ukraine.

Trees
26,000 trees grow in the park.

American Museum of Natural History
With a total floor area of 190,000 m², the museum contains over 33 million specimens.

Columbus Circle
The monument to Christopher Columbus is 'Mile Zero' – the point from which official highway distances to the city are measured.

Strawberry Fields
This peaceful area is dedicated to John Lennon, who was living in an apartment adjacent to this spot when he was shot dead on the steps of his home in 1980.

Bow Bridge
This is the largest bridge in the park (27 m long). Many movies have used it as a picturesque backdrop.

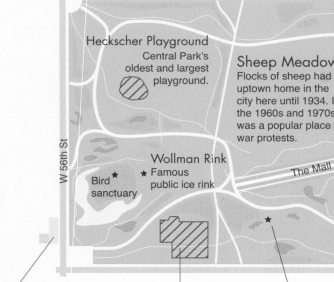

Heckscher Playground
Central Park's oldest and largest playground.

Sheep Meadow
Flocks of sheep had an uptown home in the city here until 1934. In the 1960s and 1970s it was a popular place for war protests.

Cherry Hill

Fire station ★

The Great Lawn
The largest lawn in the park covers an area 0.22 km² and is actually a turfed-over decommissioned reservoir.

Wollman Rink
★ Famous public ice rink

Bird sanctuary ★

The Mall

METROPOLITAN MUSEUM OF

5th Ave

THE PLAZA

Balto Statue
Balto the sled dog is known for his heroic delivery of diphtheria antitoxin to the sick in Alaska during a fierce blizzard in 1925.

Cleopatra's Needle
Carved in 1475 BCE, the Egyptian obelisk stands 21 m (69 ft) high and weighs about 200 tonnes. It was gifted by the British to the USA in 1881.

Central Park Zoo
Home to over 130 species of creature, from tiny leafcutter ants to giant grizzly bears.

Size
It is only the fifth-largest park in New York City but it is almost twice as large as the city-state of Monaco. Walking a full circuit of Central Park takes 2 hours.

Raccoons
At least 400 urban raccoons live in the park and can often be seen at night.

Largest crowd
Country rock superstar Garth Brooks' concert on North Meadow in 1997 drew an audience of 980,000 fans.

Old country inspiration
Frederick Law Olmsted was impressed by Birkenhead Park in England when he visited in 1850. Eight years later he won the competition to design Central Park and replicated many of its features.

Traverses
Four roads cross the park. They were planned in 1857 when the only traffic was horses and carriages.

Manhattan
The park covers 6 per cent of the total land area of Manhattan.

Summit Rock
The highest point in Central Park. Before the city was built up you could see New Jersey from here.

Central Park Tennis Center
Locals, visitors and famous tennis players including Andre Agassi and Bjorn Borg have enjoyed playing on these 30 outdoor tennis courts set amid mature trees.

The Blockhouse
This small fort is Central Park's second oldest structure (1814) and the last relic of northern Manhattan's fortifications.

Central Park West

Great Hill

Jacqueline Kennedy Onassis Reservoir
This disused reservoir, popular with joggers and waterbirds, covers 106 acres (43 ha) and holds over 1 billion gallons (3,800,000 m³) of water. Run around its perimeter 17 times and you will have completed a marathon!

North Meadow
This spacious area has 12 pitches for baseball, softball, football and other sports.

Butterfly Gardens ★

W 110 St

East Meadow

Harlem Meer

Museum Mile
The section of 5th Avenue from 82nd to 105th street is one of the world's densest concentrations of culture. There are nine major museums and many other landmarks.

Conservatory Garden
Central Park's only formal garden was opened to the public in 1937, but fell into ruin after the Second World War. It was lovingly restored in 1987 and is now a beautiful, serene corner of the world.

Lasker Pool
This open-air public swimming pool is free to use. In winter it is used for ice skating.

SOLOMON R. GUGGENHEIM MUSEUM

Duke Ellington Circle
Named after the legendary jazz musician who lived in New York City and performed at the famous Cotton Club in nearby Harlem.

THE PLAZA
One of the most famous
hotels in the world.

First in
Alfred Gwyne Vanderbilt,
of the famous Vanderbilt
family was the first guest
to arrive at the hotel.

Silver screen
The Plaza has featured in a range
of motion pictures like Alfred
Hitchcock's North by Northwest and
Baz Lurhrman's The Great Gatsby.

Demolition
The Plaza originally opened in the
1890s but was demolished in 1905 to
build a bigger premises, and become
the iconic building we know.

Trump
Donald Trump purchased
The Plaza in 1988, but
was forced by his lenders
to sell it in 1995, due to
the fact that he was on
the edge of bankruptcy.

French influence
Built in a château-style
inspired by the French
Renaissance.

Exhibitions
Solomon R. Guggenheim
debuted his first public
exhibition in his private
room at The Plaza.

Persian Room
The Persian Room is known
for hosting the best of the
best performers. In her early
years Liza Minnelli, was
frequently showcased there.

76 m
(249 ft)
(19 floors)

Room rate
When it opened in 1907, rooms were
$2.50/night – equivalent to about $60/night
now. Today, rooms range from $800/night
to $30,000/night for the Royal Plaza suite.

All about the music
The Beatles wrote *Michelle*
and Miles Davis recorded
an album here.

METROPOLITAN MUSEUM OF ART
With 7 million visitors annually, the 'Met' is the largest art museum in the USA.

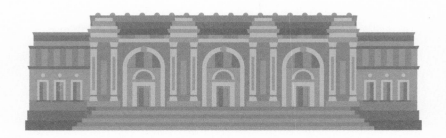

1938
The first branch of The Metropolitan Museum of Art was named 'The Met Cloisters' and it opened it 1938.

On display
There are more than two million works on display, including paintings, sculptures, musical instruments, costumes, antique weapons and armour.

The Met Gala
The museum is home to The Met Gala, an annual fundraising event that attracts some of the most famous people in the world, who often attend wearing controversial fashion. Attendees include the likes of Donatella Versace, Rihanna and Idris Elba.

Not just paintings
The world's oldest surviving piano can be found here.

SOLOMON R. GUGGENHEIM MUSEUM
This icon of 20th-century architecture exhibits modern and contemporary art.

SOLOMON R. GUGGENHEIM
$ The founder of the museum was an American businessman and art collector who made his fortune out of gold mines in Alaska.

FRANK LLOYD WRIGHT
Lloyd Wright was the designer of the Guggenheim museum and is considered one of the greatest American architects of all time. It was his last major work and opened to the public six months after his death.

In 2008 it was designated a National Historic Landmark, and was nominated to be included in the UNESCO World Heritage list in 2015.

GOLDEN GATE BRIDGE

San Francisco, USA

Construction: 4 years (1933–1937)

The Golden Gate Bridge is a famous symbol of San Francisco and the United States, and is the most photographed bridge in the world. The bridge is also a phenomenal work of architecture and engineering: it was the tallest and the longest suspension bridge in the world when it opened and was later named a wonder of the modern world.

Etymology

The bridge is named after the Golden Gate Strait, which got its name in 1846 when explorer John Fremont wrote about how it reminded him of another narrow harbour – the Golden Horn of the Bosporus in north-west Turkey.

Wonder of the modern world

The American Society of Civil Engineers named the bridge as one of their Seven Wonders of the Modern World.

High and mighty

The Golden Gate Bridge was both the tallest and the longest suspension bridge in the world at the time of its opening in 1937. Its main span is 1,280 m (4,200 ft) long and its towers are 227 m (746 ft) high. Today it remains the tallest bridge in the USA.

Colour

The colour of the bridge is officially called 'international orange'. This hue was chosen because it complements the natural surroundings and enhances the bridge's visibility in fog.

Project cost

The bridge cost around $35 million to build, which is equivalent to approximately $3.5 billion today.

Film favourite

The bridge's cinematic credits include *Superman, Vertigo, The Maltese Falcon, Godzilla* and *A View To A Kill*. It was also replicated in the top-selling video game Grand Theft Auto: *San Andreas*.

Riveting stuff

Construction of the bridge used 1.2 million steel rivets. In the 1970s many corroded rivets were replaced with modern bolts. Today there is a lively market for the original rivets that were removed.

Marin Tower

227 m

318.9 m Compared height of the Chrysler Building

1,280 m

67 m

Foundation

It took two years to complete the 53 m (175 ft) tall foundation of the south tower.

Surf spot

Sometimes surfers enjoy excellent waves here, although sharks can be a worry: 11 species call the bay home, and the fearsome Great White also swims offshore along the coast.

Earthquake resistant
On October 17, 1989 the Bay Area was hit by an earthquake measuring 6.9 on the Richter scale, the most devastating since 1906. The Golden Gate Bridge was undamaged.

Half Way to Hell Club
This was established by workers who fell from the bridge during its construction but were saved by the safety net that was strung underneath.

Maximum capacity
An all-time record of 162,414 vehicles crossed the bridge in one day on October 27, 1989.

Speed limit
The bridge has six lanes of traffic and vehicles must stick to a speed limit of 45 mph (72 km/h).

Strong winds
Golden Gate Bridge has only been closed three times due to bad weather. In 1951, 1982 and 1983 wind speeds of 111, 113 and 121 km/h respectively forced shutdowns.

North Tower

Battery Spencer
From the early 1900s to the Second World War, the battery was a working military installation and one of the main fortifications protecting San Francisco harbour.

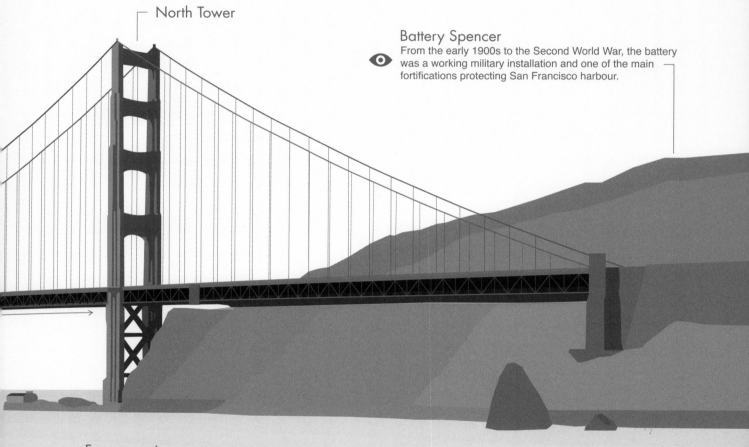

Ferry crossing
Before the completion of the bridge it took 20 minutes to cross the bay by boat.

Bridge Walk
The bridge was deliberately closed for a special 50th anniversary walk on May 24, 1987 from 4:30 am to 10:30 am.

What harbour?
European explorers, including the legendary Sir Francis Drake, sailed right past the Golden Gate Strait for two centuries without spotting it. This may have been bad luck: the opening is narrow, and the whole area is prone to thick fogs.

KENNEDY SPACE CENTER

Florida, USA
Construction: 1962

Since 1968, the Kennedy Space Center has been NASA's main launch centre for human spaceflight.

Located on Merritt Island, approximately one hour's drive from the tourist hotspot of Orlando, the centre is a popular attraction for international visitors.

Name
The centre was named in 1963 after John F. Kennedy, who two years earlier announced an ambitious plan of landing a man on the Moon by the end of the decade. This plan was achieved in 1969.

Area
The centre covers 580 km² of land (slightly larger than the Isle of Man) and houses over 700 buildings. Around 13,100 people work here.

Shuttle Landing Facility
This served as the main airport for Space Shuttles from 1981–2011.

Apollo 11
The Saturn V rocket carrying the Apollo 11 mission took off from Pad A on July 16, 1969. Four days later, Neil Armstrong and Buzz Aldrin became the first humans on the Moon.

Vehicle Assembly Building
At 160 m (526 ft) tall, 218.2 m (716 ft) long and 157.9 m (518 ft) wide, this is one of the largest buildings in the world by volume. Saturn V rockets and Space Shuttles were assembled inside before being moved on a mobile platform to the launch site.

Operations and Checkout Building
This contains crew dormitories and the rooms where they suited-up for spaceflights.

SpaceX launch complexes
Launch complex 39 is leased by the company SpaceX to launch their Falcon 9 and Falcon Heavy rockets. It has three launch pads.

Project Gemini
Rocket launch site of NASA's second manned spaceflight program (1961–1966) that developed techniques later used in the Apollo program.

Kennedy Space Center Visitor Complex
The complex was visited by over 1.7 million tourists in 2016.

SpaceX Landing Zone
Landing facility for SpaceX reusable rockets.

NASA (National Aeronautics and Space Administration)
Founded in 1958, the independent US Government agency is responsible for the national space flight program and aerospace research. It employs 17,336 people and has a budget of $21.5 billion (0.49 per cent of US Government expenditure).

Mercury-Redstone 3
Launch site of the 1961 spaceflight that made Alan Shepard the first American in space.

NASA field centres
Kennedy Space Center is one of NASA's 10 field centres and has been its primary launch centre for man missions since 1968.

Port Canaveral
With 4.2 million passengers disembarking here annually, this is the world's second-busiest cruise port.

SPACE SHUTTLE COLUMBIA
This was the first of five spaceworthy shuttles to be built. It flew 27 successful missions.

Space Shuttle program
NASA's fourth human spaceflight program was the first to feature reusable manned space vehicles. From 1981 to 2011 five orbiters, *Columbia, Challenger, Discovery, Atlantis* and *Endeavour* transported 355 people from 16 different countries into space at a cost of $196 billion.

External fuel tank
Filled with nearly 2 million litres of liquid oxygen and hydrogen used as fuel for the shuttle's engines. After 510 seconds of burn time it was jettisoned, re-entered the atmosphere and broke up into pieces before falling into the Pacific or Indian Oceans.

Disaster
In 2003, *Columbia* disintegrated during re-entry, killing all seven crew members. It was the second loss of a shuttle in the program's 113 flights.

Cause of the accident
During the launch, fragments of foam fell from the outer tank of the shuttle and punched a 25 cm hole in the thermal cover of the shuttle wing. This vulnerability was known about during the mission, but engineers were unable to see if the damage was serious enough to need radical action such as sending a second shuttle into orbit.

Deaths
The crew were two women and five men. Six were American, one was Israeli.

Distance travelled
During its 28 missions, the shuttle travelled 201,497,772 km (125 million miles) and spent a total of 300 days in space.

Solid rocket boosters
Two reusable solid-propellant rockets provided primary propulsion of the shuttle, helping it to lift off. After 127 seconds of burn time they were jettisoned, their parachutes opened and the engines fell into the Atlantic Ocean.

Crew
Columbia could carry up to eight astronauts.

Cargo bay
18 m-long payload bay used to transport artificial satellites and other cargos such as spacelabs.

Name
Named after the *Columbia Rediviva*, the first American ship to circumnavigate the globe in 1790.

Landing
The shuttle gradually lowered its orbit to re-enter the atmosphere and transition from spacecraft to aircraft. The thickening atmospheric layers heated the hull to over 1,500 °C. It landed on a runway at 346 km/h (215 mph) and used a parachute to brake.

Reusable engines
The three main engines of the shuttle could gimbal 10.5 degrees up and down, and 8.5 degrees from side to side to steer the shuttle.

NASA

Columbia

PENTAGON

Virginia, USA
Construction: 2 years (1941–1943)

The Pentagon is the headquarters of the United States Department of Defense and it is the largest office building in the world. It is also aptly named: it has five sides, five floors above ground level and five corridors running round each floor. It even has five food courts.

'The Pentagon' is frequently used as a metonym for the Department of Defense and the leadership of the US military. The building's historical and architectural significance have earned it a place on the National Register of Historic Places and it is recognised as a National Historic Landmark.

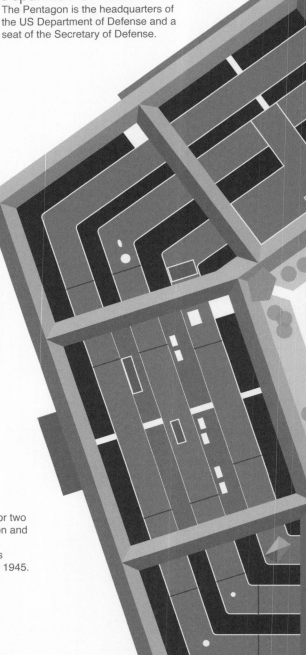

Pentagon station
The Pentagon has its own station served by two Washington Metro lines. It's used by 13,989 passengers daily (2016).

Department of Defense
The Pentagon is the headquarters of the US Department of Defense and a seat of the Secretary of Defense.

Largest office building
It's the largest office building in the world with approximately. 600,000 m² of space and is 1.3 times larger than its nearest rival, Place du Portage in Canada.

Construction cost
It's construction cost at the time of its completion was $83 million, which was the equivalent of around $1.1 billion in 2018.

Employees
Around 26,000 people work here.

Racial segregation
At the time of its completion, Virginia state law enforced racial segregation in all public buildings. However, Executive Order 8802 from 1941 abolished discrimination in the American defence industry.

Leslie Groves
This Lieutenant General was responsible for two major projects: construction of the Pentagon and development of the Manhattan Project, the operation that developed the atomic bombs detonated over Hiroshima and Nagasaki in 1945.

Facilities
The building includes 9 basketball courts, 284 toilets, 691 drinking fountains, 7,754 windows, and meditation and prayer rooms.

Pentagon road network
A new highway system was specifically built to improve employees' journeys to the Pentagon.

Parking
A huge car park in front of the building covers 27 hectares and has a capacity of 8,770 vehicles.

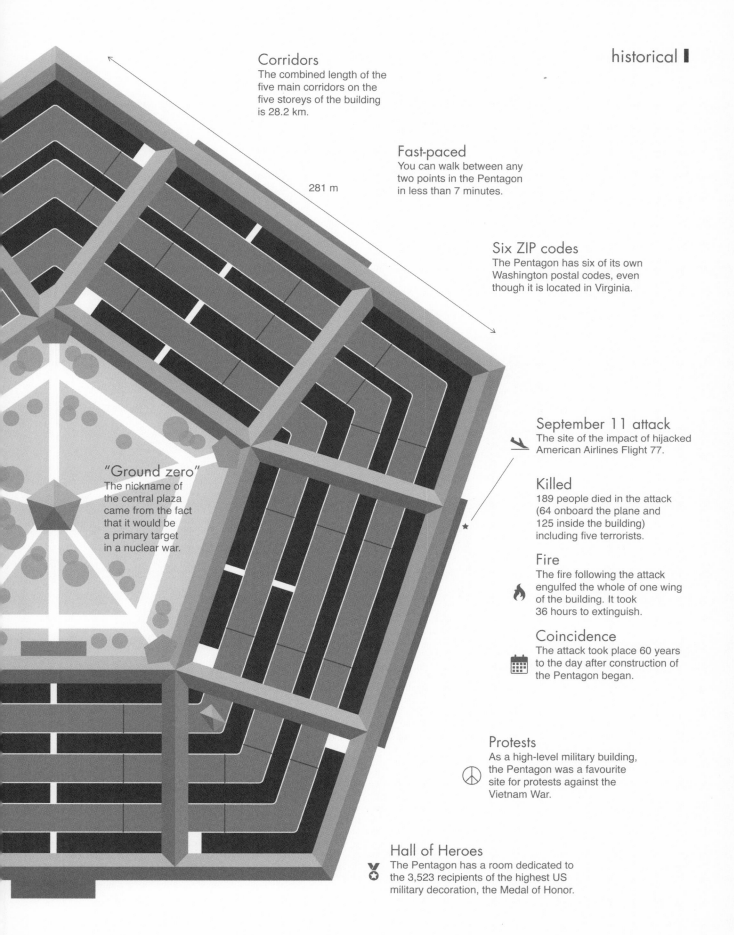

Corridors
The combined length of the five main corridors on the five storeys of the building is 28.2 km.

281 m

Fast-paced
You can walk between any two points in the Pentagon in less than 7 minutes.

Six ZIP codes
The Pentagon has six of its own Washington postal codes, even though it is located in Virginia.

"Ground zero"
The nickname of the central plaza came from the fact that it would be a primary target in a nuclear war.

September 11 attack
The site of the impact of hijacked American Airlines Flight 77.

Killed
189 people died in the attack (64 onboard the plane and 125 inside the building) including five terrorists.

Fire
The fire following the attack engulfed the whole of one wing of the building. It took 36 hours to extinguish.

Coincidence
The attack took place 60 years to the day after construction of the Pentagon began.

Protests
As a high-level military building, the Pentagon was a favourite site for protests against the Vietnam War.

Hall of Heroes
The Pentagon has a room dedicated to the 3,523 recipients of the highest US military decoration, the Medal of Honor.

STATUE OF LIBERTY

New York City, USA

Construction: 9 years (1877–1886)

A gift from France to the American people, the Statue of Liberty is a unique symbol of freedom and independence. Completed in 1886, it was built to commemorate the Declaration of Independence 110 years before and the recent abolition of slavery. For millions of emigrants coming to New York it was the first landmark they saw in their new homeland. The statue became a symbol of the new life they would enjoy in America.

Ellis Island
This island, just 0.7 km away from the statue, was once the main immigrant inspection station for arrivals from Europe. Over 12 million people became Americans on this tiny piece of land.

Oysters aplenty
The tidal areas around the island and the western side of the bay were once covered with huge oyster beds which were a valued food for the Lenape people and were enjoyed for centuries more by New Yorkers.

Bedloe's Island
For many years the island was named after Isaac Bedloe, who bought it in 1667. It was renamed Liberty Island in 1956.

Quarantine
In the 18th century, the island was commandeered by the city for use as a smallpox quarantine station.

LIBERTY ISLAND

New Jersey – 0.6 km

Manhattan – 2.5 km

Ferry dock

STATUE OF LIBERTY

Fort Wood
Built in 1811 to protect New York from a possible British invasion, by the 1880s the fort was obsolete and disused. Its formidable star-shaped walls were adapted into an ideal base for the statue.

Welcome
The statue was a welcome sight to the millions of immigrants who arrived in the US by ship in the late 19th and 20th centuries.

Tickets
The ferry to the island costs $18.50. It is an additional $3 to make the journey up to the tiara observation point – but it's very much worth it!

Exclave
Liberty Island lies in the waters of the state of New Jersey. However, it was declared an exclave of the island of Manhattan and officially belongs to New York.

Personal experience
The designer of the statue sailed past this island during his trip to America and this was the moment he chose it as a location.

Dedication
As many as a million people attended the parade and ceremony of dedication for the statue in 1886. As the parade passed the stock exchange, workers threw ticker tape from the windows, starting the tradition of the New York ticker-tape parade.

Liberty Enlightening the World
Official name of the statue
(French: La Liberté éclairant le monde)

Designer
The statue was designed by Frédéric Auguste Bartholdi and constructed by Gustave Eiffel, creator of his namesake tower in Paris.

Fundraising
The statue's torch-bearing arm and head were constructed before the overall design was complete and were displayed for fundraising. The mammoth scale of the statue captured the public's imagination and over 120,000 people donated money.

Construction
The monument was first built in France then deconstructed and shipped across the ocean in parts.

Curtain wall construction
The statue was one of the first structures to have an outer covering that is not load-bearing and instead be supported by the interior framework.

"The New Colossus"
'Give me your tired, your poor, your huddled masses yearning to breathe free' – these famous lines come from the sonnet *The New Colossus*, written by American poet Emma Lazarus to help raise funds for the construction of the monument.

Torch
Until 1916 visitors could climb up to the balcony around the torch on a single 40 ft (12 m) long ladder that runs through the arm.

View from the top
The observation deck is sited just under the statue's tiara, which has seven spikes representing the world's seven continents.

Tabula ansata
In her left hand Liberty holds a tablet showing the date of the US Declaration of Independence (July 4, 1776) inscribed in Roman numerals 'JULY IV MDCCLXXVI'.

Roman goddess
The statue presents the figure of Libertas, Roman goddess of liberty.

Broken chain
Liberty is actually in the process of stepping over a broken chain, which symbolises gaining freedom. Her upraised heel can clearly be seen from the rear of the statue.

Restoration
The statue has been restored three times: in 1938, 1984–1986 and 2011–2012.

WHITE HOUSE

Washington, USA
Construction: 8 years (1792–1800)

The White House is a world-famous symbol of Washington, the United States and the office of the President. The building is a popular example of neoclassical architecture. It has featured in hundreds of movies and several TV series have been set within its walls. Every US president has lived here since John Adams in 1800.

Name change
The complex was known as the 'Executive Residence' until 1901 when it was changed during the presidency of Theodore Roosevelt.

Address
The White House's address, 1600 Pennsylvania Avenue NW, Washington, D.C., is probably the most famous address in the world.

President's Park
The White House is surrounded by a 313,536 m² park, which is managed by the National Park Service.

West Wing
Office space for the president's executive office staff. The Cabinet Room, the Situation Room, the Roosevelt Room and the White House press corps are all located here.

Rooms
The White House has 132 rooms and 35 bathrooms. The complex has a chocolate shop, a music room and a bowling alley.

Oval Office
The White House's most famous room is the main workplace of the President.

East Wing
This has office space for the First Lady and her staff. The visitors' entrance is located here.

Swimming pool
Installed in 1975 by President Gerald Ford.

Grassy helipad
The President's helicopter, Marine One, lands on the middle of the South Lawn.

Jogging track
President Bill Clinton ordered the installation of a quarter-mile long jogging track around the White House so that he could go running without disrupting traffic in the city.

Vegetable garden
First Lady Michelle Obama created an organic vegetable garden and installed a beehive on the South Lawn.

Banknote
The White House features on the reverse of the $20 bill.

National Christmas Tree
Since 1923 a Christmas tree has been placed here. It is traditionally lit by the President.

Press Center

White House Theater

EXECUTIVE RESIDENCE

Rose Garden

Kennedy Garden

The White House South Lawn

Basketball court

EXECUTIVE RESIDENCE
The main building of the White House complex is the home of the head of state.

Electricity
The White House was lit by gas lamps until it was electrified in 1891.

American flag
Its 50 stars represent the country's 50 states and the 13 red and white stripes represent the thirteen colonies that signed the Declaration of Independence in 1776.

Bulletproof windows
All the windows have bullet-proof glass.

Truman Balcony
This was added in 1948, during the presidency of Harry S. Truman.

Lincoln Bedroom
Today this is a guest suite. Abraham Lincoln used it as his office.

2nd floor & attic
Private living space for the President's family.

President's bedroom

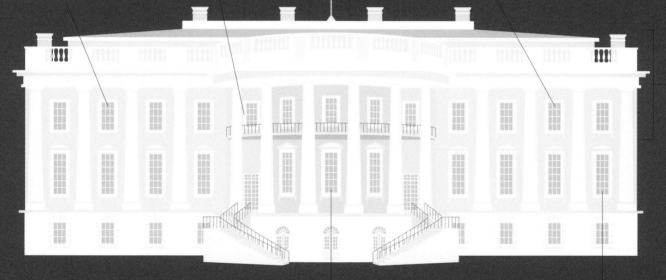

Basement
There are rooms here for the White House carpenters, engineers, flower designer and dentist.

Blue Room
This has been blue since 1837. It's used for welcoming state visitors and for small dinners.

East Room
A large banqueting hall.

Security
The White House is protected by the Secret Service and the United States Park Police.

Closed airspace
Airspace around the White House is strictly prohibited to all aircraft. The White House is protected by surface-to-air missiles.

Deaths
Two Presidents and three First Ladies have died in the White House.

WORLD TRADE CENTER

Manhattan, New York City, USA
Construction: 6 years (1967–1973)

The World Trade Center will always be known for the tragic events of September 11, 2001. However, it also goes down in history for the remarkable design and innovative construction of the Twin Towers.

At the time of their completion in 1973, the Twin Towers were the tallest buildings in the world. The South Tower stood at 415.1 m (1,362 ft); its partner was slight taller at 417 m (1,368 ft). The South Tower had more floors (110) than any other building in the world, a record that was not surpassed until the Burj Khalifa opened in 2010.

"The walk"
In 1974, high-wire artist Philippe Petit sneaked into the building and strung a cable between the two towers. He walked from tower to tower eight times, to the cheers of the crowd below.

South Tower

North Tower

Second impact
United Airlines Flight 175, with 65 people onboard hit the South Tower at 9:03 a.m. The tower collapsed 56 minutes later.

Stairwell A
The plane's impact cut off all three of the North Tower's stairwells. In the South Tower, two were cut. Stairwell A narrowly avoided destruction and 18 people on the floors of impact or above were able to evacuate.

9/11
In 2001 the deadliest terrorist attack in world history struck the towers. Two hijacked planes were flown into the buildings, killing 2,606 people.

First impact
American Airlines Flight 11, with 92 people onboard, hit the North Tower at 8:46 a.m. The tower collapsed 102 minutes later.

The only video
There was only one accurate recording of the first plane hitting the North Tower.

24

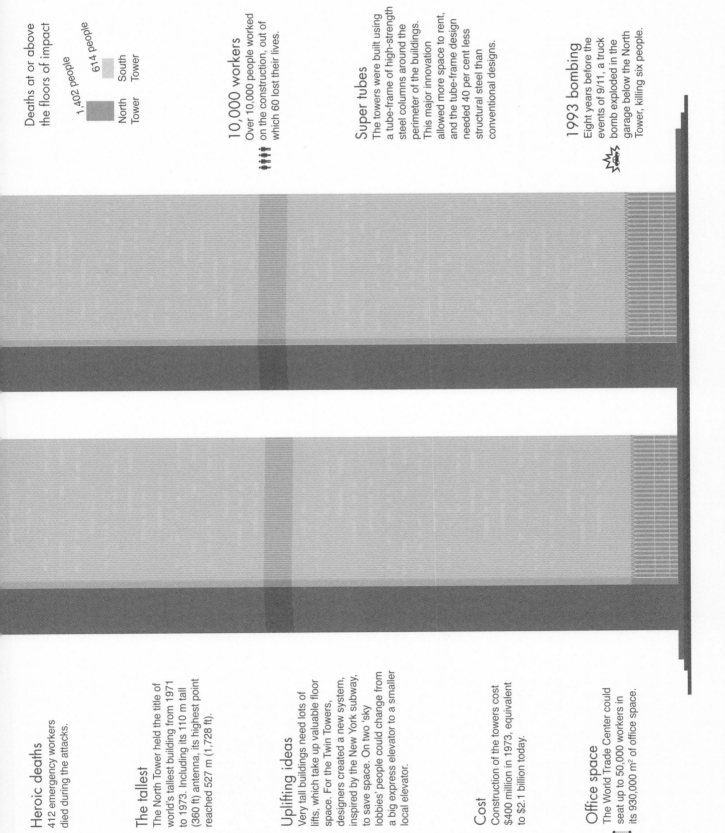

Deaths at or above the floors of impact

1,402 people — North Tower
614 people — South Tower

10,000 workers
Over 10,000 people worked on the construction, out of which 60 lost their lives.

Super tubes
The towers were built using a tube-frame of high-strength steel columns around the perimeter of the buildings. This major innovation allowed more space to rent, and the tube-frame design needed 40 per cent less structural steel than conventional designs.

1993 bombing
Eight years before the events of 9/11, a truck bomb exploded in the garage below the North Tower, killing six people.

Heroic deaths
412 emergency workers died during the attacks.

The tallest
The North Tower held the title of world's tallest building from 1971 to 1973. Including its 110 m tall (360 ft) antenna, its highest point reached 527 m (1,728 ft).

Uplifting ideas
Very tall buildings need lots of lifts, which take up valuable floor space. For the Twin Towers, designers created a new system, inspired by the New York subway, to save space. On two 'sky lobbies' people could change from a big express elevator to a smaller local elevator.

Cost
Construction of the towers cost $400 million in 1973, equivalent to $2.1 billion today.

Office space
The World Trade Center could seat up to 50,000 workers in its 930,000 m² of office space.

ONE WORLD
TRADE CENTER

Manhattan, New York City
Construction: 8 years (2006–2014)

One World Trade Center only opened in 2014, but is already considered an iconic landmark on the New York skyline.

The building prides itself on the collaboration opportunities and community growth it offers to its tenants. It is home to a vibrant mix of organisations, ranging from startup businesses to leading global brands.

The structure was built where the North Tower of the original World Trade Center stood. The building's safety features have been developed far beyond the NYC building code, and it is now known as one of the safest buildings in the world.

1,776 ft
The height from the ground to the tip of the spire was deliberately chosen to be 1,776 ft – to match the year in which the United States Declaration of Independence was written.

North American Giant
One World Trade Center is the tallest building in North America and the Western Hemisphere, and is the sixth-tallest in the world.

417 m
The building is exactly the same height as the original North Tower.

One World Observatory
Visitors are whisked up to the viewing area in just 47 seconds. Thanks to its position in Lower Manhattan, the Observatory offers an unbeatable view of the Statue of Liberty.

Freedom Tower
This was the former name of the building before it officially changed to 'One World Trade Center' in 2009.

Safety
The new building was designed to be the safest in the world.

Cost
The estimated construction cost in 2012 was $3.9 billion, making it then the world's most expensive building.

Obama's inscription

President Barack Obama wrote, 'We remember, we rebuild, we come back stronger!' on a steel beam at the top of the tower.

Elevators

The building has 71 lifts. It takes them less than 60 seconds to reach the top, travelling at the same speed as Usain Bolt running flat out.

Cornerstone

This was laid in 2004 by New York City Mayor Michael Bloomberg and its inscription reads, 'The enduring spirit of freedom'.

World Trade Center Site Plan

One WTC

North Pool

Museum

South Pool

Survivor Tree

A small pear tree was discovered under the rubble after the towers came down. Against all odds, it later resprouted. After its symbolic recovery, the tree now grows at the site memorial.

Memorial pools

Two reflecting pools now mark the footprints of the fallen towers. The pools feature the largest man-made waterfalls on the continent.

Concrete base

The new building stands on a 56 m (174 ft) tall concrete base, protecting it against any ground-level attacks.

Each hand of the Christ the Redeemer statue weighs 8 tonnes and is marked with crucifixion wounds.

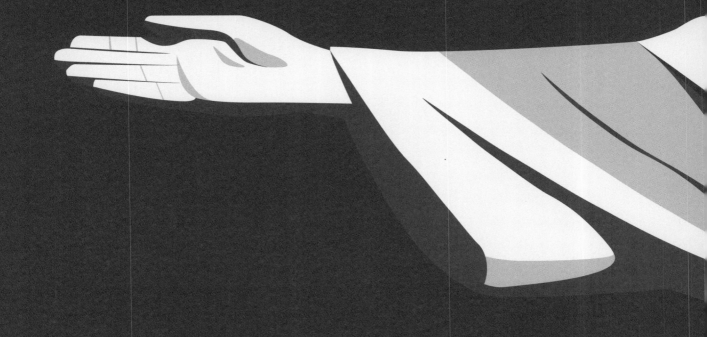

BRASÍLIA

Federal District, Brazil
Construction: founded 1960

Brasília is a masterpiece of modernist architecture and town planning. It was conceived as a new, purpose-built federal capital city and was the realisation of a long-held national dream for a capital at the heart of the country.

Its districts and neighbourhoods are laid out in a symmetrical pattern around a grand central avenue by the shore of a man-made lake. The city has many iconic public buildings designed by renowned Brazilian architect Oscar Niemeyer. Brasília was recognised by UNESCO in 2017 as a 'City of Design'.

Foundation
The city was founded in 1960 as a new, purpose-built city to replace Rio de Janeiro as the capital.

Heart of the country
In 1891, Brazil's first republican constitution stated that the capital should be moved from the heavily populated coast to a more central location.

World Heritage Site
In 1987, the city was added to the UNESCO World Heritage Site list for its outstanding universal value.

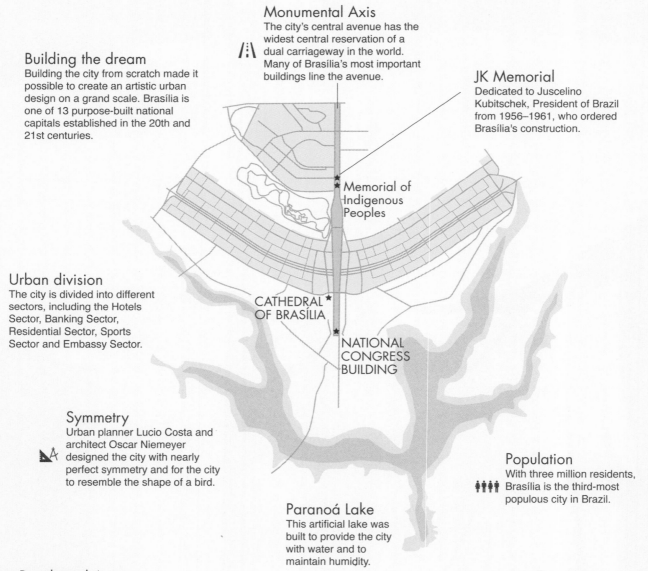

Monumental Axis
The city's central avenue has the widest central reservation of a dual carriageway in the world. Many of Brasília's most important buildings line the avenue.

Building the dream
Building the city from scratch made it possible to create an artistic urban design on a grand scale. Brasília is one of 13 purpose-built national capitals established in the 20th and 21st centuries.

JK Memorial
Dedicated to Juscelino Kubitschek, President of Brazil from 1956–1961, who ordered Brasília's construction.

Memorial of Indigenous Peoples

CATHEDRAL OF BRASÍLIA

NATIONAL CONGRESS BUILDING

Urban division
The city is divided into different sectors, including the Hotels Sector, Banking Sector, Residential Sector, Sports Sector and Embassy Sector.

Symmetry
Urban planner Lucio Costa and architect Oscar Niemeyer designed the city with nearly perfect symmetry and for the city to resemble the shape of a bird.

Population
With three million residents, Brasília is the third-most populous city in Brazil.

Paranoá Lake
This artificial lake was built to provide the city with water and to maintain humidity.

Residential Axis
The residential sector of the city consists of 108 superblocks designed to be self-sufficient neighbourhoods.

Economy
The city has the highest GDP per capita ($21,779) of all Latin American cities.

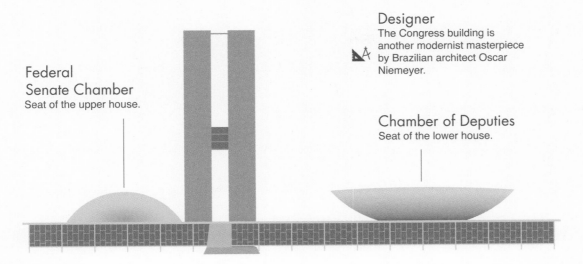

Federal Senate Chamber
Seat of the upper house.

Designer
The Congress building is another modernist masterpiece by Brazilian architect Oscar Niemeyer.

Chamber of Deputies
Seat of the lower house.

Going underground
Some of the buildings of the National Congress are connected by tunnels.

Location
The National Congress building is in the centre of the city's Monumental Axis.

CATHEDRAL OF BRASÍLIA
This is one of the most beautiful buildings of the new capital city. The striking concrete and glass roof seems to be opening up to heaven.

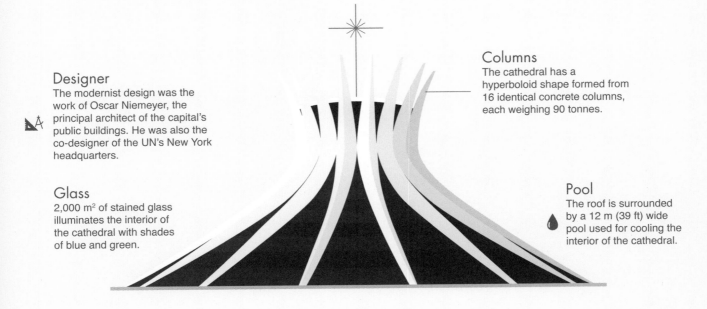

Columns
The cathedral has a hyperboloid shape formed from 16 identical concrete columns, each weighing 90 tonnes.

Designer
The modernist design was the work of Oscar Niemeyer, the principal architect of the capital's public buildings. He was also the co-designer of the UN's New York headquarters.

Glass
2,000 m² of stained glass illuminates the interior of the cathedral with shades of blue and green.

Pool
The roof is surrounded by a 12 m (39 ft) wide pool used for cooling the interior of the cathedral.

Entrance
To enter, you walk through a dark tunnel under the pool and step out into the bright, illuminated interior.

Hidden beauty
Most of the cathedral is below ground, with the base of the 70 m (230 ft) roof structure at ground level.

RIO DE JANEIRO

Brazil

Construction: founded 1565

Rio de Janeiro is one of the most-visited cities in the southern hemisphere. In 2017, Rio de Janeiro was awarded World Heritage cultural site status by UNESCO, with particular recognition as the first urban cultural landscape to earn that honour. The city's stunning natural environment includes lagoons, beaches, steep mountains, islands and a lush rainforest. The city itself is an energetic mix of fine architecture, beautiful parks and vibrant local neighbourhoods.

Architecture
Rio de Janeiro was chosen as UNESCO's first World Capital of Architecture and will receive the honour in 2020.

Sugarloaf Mountain
To reach the summit you can take a spectacular cable car or rock-climb. The many steep mountains around Rio make it one of the largest urban climbing areas in the world.

Corcovado
This is the 710 m (2,330 ft) high mountain that Christ the Redeemer stands atop. Its name means 'hunchback' in Portuguese.

Tijuca Forest
This tropical rainforest is the largest urban forest in the world, covering an area of over 32 km² (12.4 sq mi).

CHRIST THE REDEMEER

Copacabana beach
One of the most famous beaches in the world, Copacabana is 4 km (2.5 miles) long and has historic forts at either end. It has been the official venue of the FIFA Beach Soccer World Cup many times.

Rodrigo de Freitas Lagoon
This is very popular for rowing and it hosted rowing and sprint canoeing events during the 2016 Summer Olympics.

Ipanema beach
This beach and its surrounding area is known for its thriving social scene made famous by the bossa nova jazz song 'Girl from Ipanema', which became a worldwide hit in the 1960s.

Jardim Botânico
This beautiful botanical garden is home to over 6,500 species, many of which are endangered. Its research centre has a superb botany library with over 32,000 volumes.

Rod rocks Rio
Rod Stewart's concert on New Year's Eve in 1994 attracted an incredible 3.5 million fans and is the highest-attended concert in history.

CHRIST THE REDEEMER

Proposals for a Christian monument here were made as early as 1850. It wasn't until 1922 that a local Catholic group managed to raise enough funds to build a statue to symbolically counter what they saw as the lack of faith in society.

Colossal saviour
The statue was completed in 1931 after nine years of construction. Christ is 30 m (98 ft) high and stands on an 8 m (26 ft) pedestal. Christ's arms are 28 m (92 ft) wide from fingertip to fingertip.

New wonder
In 2007 the statue was included in the New Seven Wonders of the World list.

Head
Christ's head has been sculpted facing downwards so that he looks down on the city. The head weighs around 30 tonnes.

Hands
Each hand weighs 8 tonnes and is marked with crucifixion wounds.

Lightning
Rio's tropical location makes it one of the world's lightning hotspots. The statue has lightning rods on top of its head and arms, but strikes can still cause damage. Shortly before the 2014 World Cup, lightning blasted off the tip of the middle finger on the right hand.

Design
The statue was designed in Art Deco style by French sculptor Paul Landowski. It is the largest Art Deco sculpture in the world. It was built by local engineer Heitor da Silva Costa.

Heart
The statue has a carved stone heart, which lies deep inside the structure, and cannot be seen from the outside.

Different designs
Early designs for the monument included Christ holding the cross in one hand and the globe in the other. The chosen design shows Christ the Redeemer with open arms, a gesture of peace and compassion.

Stone tiles
Around 6 million soapstone tiles were imported from Sweden to add a beautiful finish to the concrete structure. Many of them have hidden messages on their backs written by workers.

Staircase
The entrance to the hidden staircase used for maintenance is roughly where Christ's right ankle would be.

Chapel
There is a small chapel inside the pedestal of the statue. In 2003 escalators, lifts and walkways were installed, making it possible to access the platform that surrounds Christ's feet.

Reinforced concrete
The statue is made of reinforced concrete and soapstone. It was built in separate pieces which were then taken to the mountain top and assembled.

Weight
The statue weighs 635 tonnes, equivalent to three blue whales.

Cost
Construction cost around $250,000, equivalent to $3,500,000 today.

Among the tallest
It is the world's sixth-tallest statue of Christ. The tallest is in Poland and is 36 m (118 ft) high. However, Rio's Christ the Redeemer has the most impressive setting.

Vandalism
In 2010, vandals sprayed paint along one of the figure's arms. They later turned themselves in to police and apologised.

MOAI

Easter Island, Chile
Construction: c.250 years (1400–1650)

For nearly three centuries, the stunning moai sculptures of Easter Island in the Pacific Ocean have captured the imaginations of explorers and visitors alike. Each of these colossal monolithic statues are carved from a single block of volcanic rock, can stand nearly 10 m tall (33 ft) and weigh up to 86 tonnes. They were probably carved to represent the ancient Polynesians' ancestors and there are around 1,000 of them lined up on the perimeter of the island. As well as the artistic beauty and mystery of the moai, erecting them must have demanded incredible ingenuity, organisation and effort.

Isolation
Easter Island is one of the most remote inhabited islands in the world. It lies 3,512 km (2,182 miles) from the continent of South America and 2,075 km (1,289 miles) from the nearest inhabited island.

Population
In 1722, the population of the island was probably 2,000–3,000 people. By 1877, due to slavery and disease introduced by European explorers, only 111 natives remained on the island.

European arrival
Dutch explorer Jacob Roggeveen was the first European to visit the island, in 1722. His expedition was met with violent local resistance.

Civil war
In 1722, most of the statues were standing. However, by 1838 almost all moai had been toppled. This was probably a result of tribal conflicts within the island's native population.

First arrivals
Polynesians probably arrived on Easter Island around the year 1200 CE . They started the construction of the moai soon afterwards.

∴ - single moai (completed)

■ - ahu platform

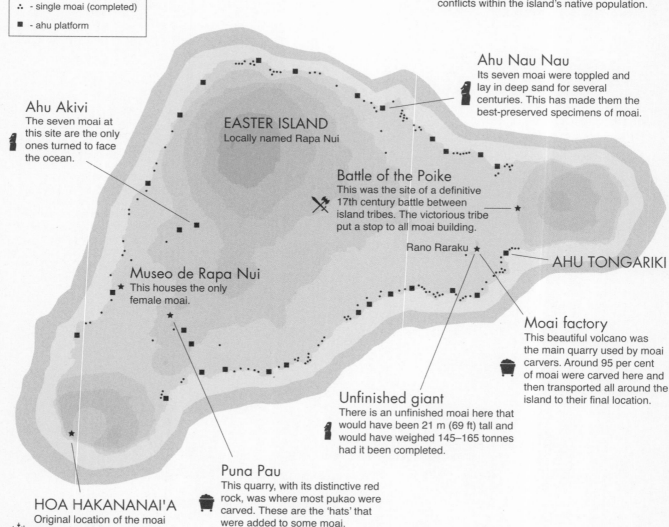

Ahu Nau Nau
Its seven moai were toppled and lay in deep sand for several centuries. This has made them the best-preserved specimens of moai.

Ahu Akivi
The seven moai at this site are the only ones turned to face the ocean.

EASTER ISLAND
Locally named Rapa Nui

Battle of the Poike
This was the site of a definitive 17th century battle between island tribes. The victorious tribe put a stop to all moai building.

Rano Raraku

AHU TONGARIKI

Museo de Rapa Nui
This houses the only female moai.

Moai factory
This beautiful volcano was the main quarry used by moai carvers. Around 95 per cent of moai were carved here and then transported all around the island to their final location.

Unfinished giant
There is an unfinished moai here that would have been 21 m (69 ft) tall and would have weighed 145–165 tonnes had it been completed.

Puna Pau
This quarry, with its distinctive red rock, was where most pukao were carved. These are the 'hats' that were added to some moai.

HOA HAKANANAI'A
Original location of the moai that was 'stolen' and shipped to Europe.

HOA HAKANANAI'A
The only moai not on the Easter Island.

"Stolen" moai
Hoa Hakananai'a was brought to England as a gift to Queen Victoria in 1869. At that time, it was one of only a few moai standing erect. It is now in the British Museum in London.

Rapa Nui people consider the statue to be stolen and demand its return.

The nose was sculpted first. It established the symmetry and proportion of each statue.

The lips were usually carved to form a thin pout.

The hands press near the base of the stomach in a sign of reverence.

2.4 m

0.96 m

Not only heads
The moai are known as the 'Easter Island heads' due to the over-large size of the head compared with the body. The name also comes from photographs of 150 heads scattered on a slope of the Rano Raraku volcano with their bodies buried underground.

Average size of moai
Average height: 4 m (13 ft)
Average width at the base: 1.6 m (5.2 ft)
Average weight: 12.5 tonnes

Volcanic origins
Almost all moai are sculpted from tuff, a compressed volcanic ash. Tuff is a relatively soft rock and is good for carving.

Sculpting time
Estimates for the time needed to create a moai vary from a couple of weeks to one year.

Watching over people
The moai were placed facing away from the ocean and towards the villages, as if their purpose was to watch over the Rapa Nui people.

Transportation
The method of moving the moai remains a mystery. One likely theory is that the statues were first roped on two sides. Teams of islanders then pulled alternately on the ropes, making the moai rock from side to side and 'walk' forwards.

Paro
'Paro' was originally the tallest moai, standing almost 10 m high and weighing 82 tonnes.

How Paro would have looked while standing.

9.8 m

Today, Paro and its pukao are toppled.

Pukao

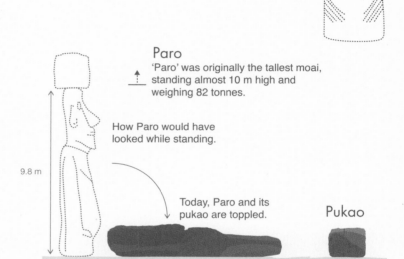

AHU TONGARIKI
This is the largest ahu on the island with 15 moai standing on it. It needed major restoration after a 1960 tsunami hit the island and swept the statues inland.

Pukao
These 'hats' made from red rock were placed on top of some moai in the 15th–16th centuries. They may represent the topknot worn by island chieftains.

Ahu
Some moai have been placed on stone platforms known as 'ahu'.

Ancient astronomy
The moai at Ahu Tongariki figures face the sunset during the summer solstice.

The heaviest
The heaviest moai ever erected weighs 86 tonnes – that's 15 tonnes heavier than the Space Shuttle.

MACHU PICCHU

Cusco Region, Peru
Construction: started c.1450

Perched on an airy mountain top surrounded by sheer cliffs, Machu Picchu is the best-preserved Inca city and an instantly recognisable icon of this advanced civilisation.

Machu Picchu was abandoned in the first half of the 16th century and only discovered by Western civilisation in 1911. Today, visitors marvel at the ingenuity and artistry of the people who built this staggering citadel in the clouds.

Its cultural value was recognised by UNESCO in 1983 when it was awarded World Heritage Site status.

Discovery
In 1911, Hiram Bingham, a Yale University lecturer, asked a local farmer if he knew any Inca ruins. The farmer led him to an abandoned city at the top of a mountain, overgrown with thick vegetation. Bingham had stumbled on one of the greatest archeological discoveries of all time.

Intihuatana stone
This ritual stone points directly at the sun during the winter solstice. It probably served as an astronomic clock or calendar.

Temple of the Three Windows
Its three windows symbolise three parts of the world: the underground (Uku-Pacha) the heaven (Hanan-Pacha) and the present (Kay-Pacha).

Quary

Funerary Rock

Cemetery

Population
Around 750 people lived here. The complex was inhabited for 80 years before being abandoned.

Legal booty
Many of the artefacts found onsite were legally taken to the Yale University Museum as Peruvian law stated that archeological discoveries belonged to the discoverer.

Reconstruction
Most of Machu Picchu's buildings were in ruins and had to be restored to give tourists a better understanding of how the citadel looked in its heyday.

Inti Mach'ay
Ritual cave used for the initiation of boys into manhood during the Royal Feast of the Sun. They had their ears pierced and watched the sunrise from the cave.

Sacred Rock

Royal Palace

Temple of the Sun
Ceremonial temple dedicated to Inti, the Inca god of the sun. During the winter solstice, sunlight entered through the central window and fell directly on a ceremonial stone.

Urubamba River

Urubamba River
A wild river runs below cliffs that drop vertically for 450 m (1,476 ft).

Abandoned city

Machu Picchu was built around 1450 but abandoned less than a century later when Spanish conquistadors invaded the continent. Despite lying only 80 km (50 miles) from the Inca capital Cusco, its high elevation (2,430 m) ensured that the citadel was never found by the Spanish. This saved it from being plundered and destroyed like many other Inca cities.

Royal estate

Machu Picchu was built as a residence for the emperor Pachacuti, who ruled the Incas from 1438 to 1472. The citadel was built to celebrate one of his successful military campaigns.

Huayna Picchu (2,693 m)

Each morning, the high priest signalled the coming of the day from the top of this mountain.

Plague theory

The population of Machu Picchu could have been wiped out by a plague of smallpox before the Spanish reached this region.

Tourists

The number of visitors grew from 80,000 in 1991 to 1,578,030 in 2018. Visits have had to be restricted to preserve the citadel.

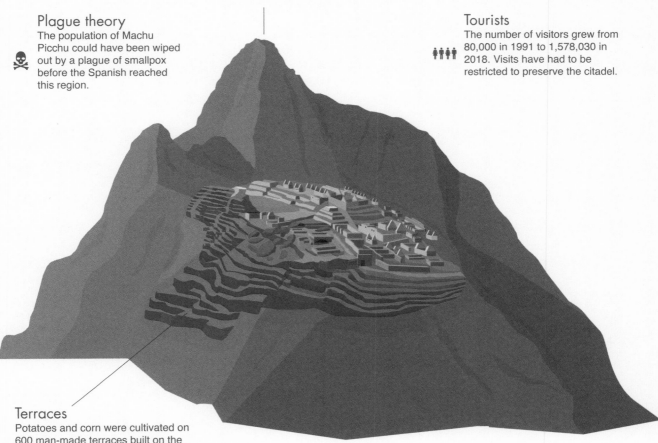

Terraces

Potatoes and corn were cultivated on 600 man-made terraces built on the steep slopes of the mountain. Their advanced construction ensured good drainage and protection from erosion. The soil was brought from the valley.

New Wonder of the World

Machu Picchu was named one of the New Seven Wonders of the World.

Advanced architecture

The stones used in building were pre-cut with extreme precision so that they fit together perfectly without mortar.

Military secret

The lofty location of the citadel gave it good natural defences and helped hide it from enemies.

When the Leaning Tower of Pisa's tilt was at its greatest, a ball dropped from the top would have landed 4.5 m (15 ft) from the base.

Europe

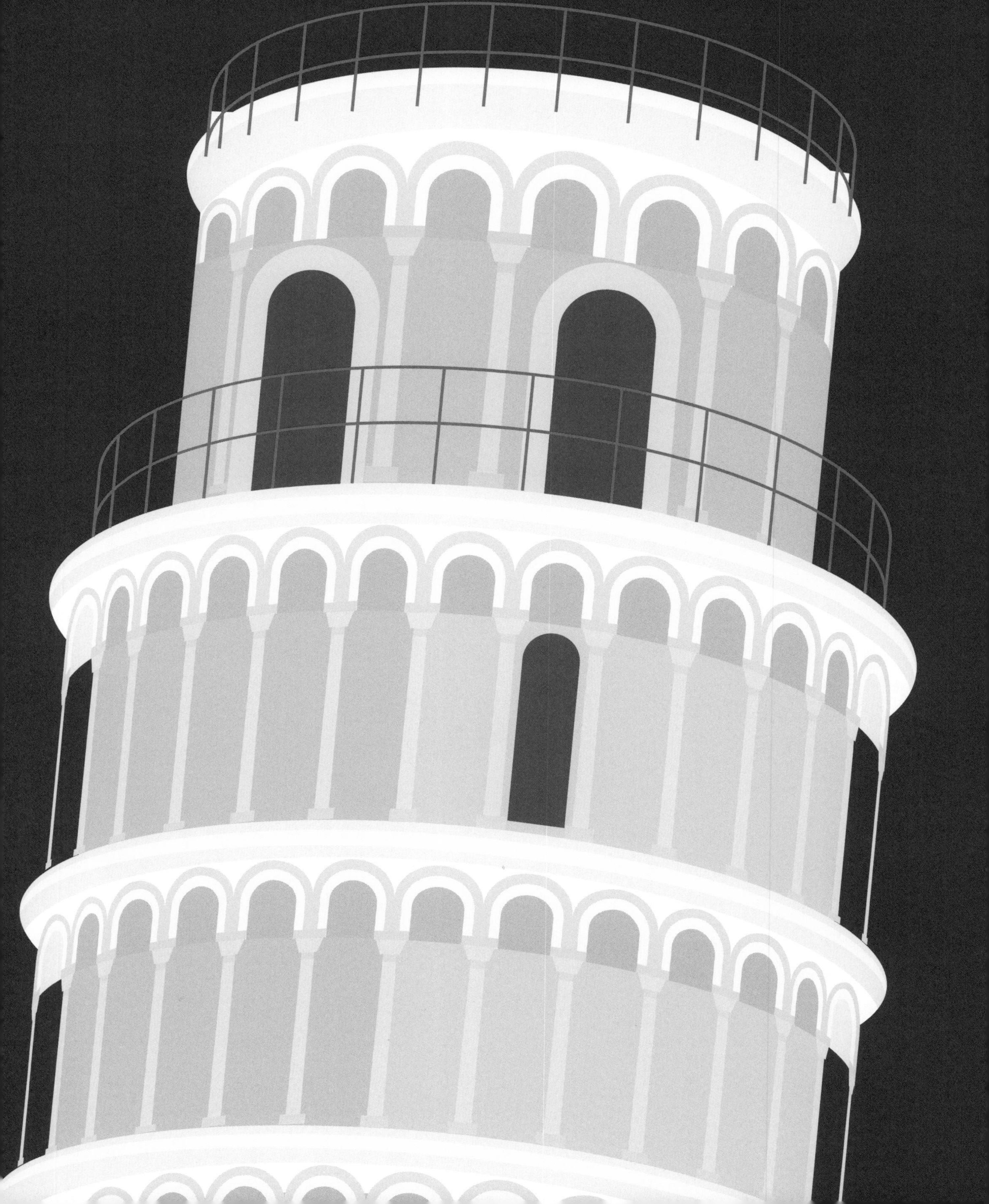

ARC DE TRIOMPHE

Paris, France

Construction: 30 years (1806–1836)

One of the most famous monuments in Paris, the arch is a symbol of France's revolutionary spirit, which greatly influenced other nations, and of its military strength. It was the tallest triumphal arch in the world for over a century. It was built on the orders of Napoleon after his victory at the Battle of Austerlitz in 1806, his greatest military achievement.

The Arc de Triomphe stands at the centre of a grand city plan of boulevards and offers one of the finest views of France's capital city from its terrace.

Location

The arch is at the hub of 12 radiating avenues at the western end of the Champs Elysées, the most famous street in Paris.

Battle of Abukir

Relief commemorating Napoleon's victory over the Ottoman army in 1799.

Design

The arch was designed by French architect Jean Chalgrin and was inspired by the 1st century Arch of Titus in Rome.

Le Triomphe de 1810

Sculpture celebrating the Treaty of Schönbrunn and the French victory over Austria during the Napoleonic Wars.

Defeats

The arch is a symbol of French victories, but German armies have twice marched under it: in 1871 during the Franco-Prussian War and in 1940 during the German occupation of Paris in the Second World War.

Commemoration of the fallen

The monument was built to commemorate soldiers who fought in the French Revolutionary Wars (1792–1802) and the Napoleonic Wars (1803–1815).

Terrace
You can enjoy a spectacular view of Paris from the top.

The tallest
For 102 years the Arc de Triomphe was the tallest triumphal arch in the world at 50 m (164 ft), until in 1938 it was overtaken by the Monumento a la Revolución in Mexico City (67 m, 220 ft).

Flight
In 1919, Charles Godefroy flew through the Arc de Triomphe in his Nieuport 27 biplane. The event was filmed by his friend.

General Marceau's burial
Relief depicting the funeral of this French general of the Revolutionary Wars who died in battle at the age of 27.

Inscriptions
The names of all major French victories and generals are inscribed on the inner and outer walls.

Le Départ de 1792
This sculpture depicts revolutionaries of the French Revolution and the personification of Liberty flying over them.

Tomb of the Unknown Soldier
Beneath the monument is the symbolic Tomb of the Unknown Soldier, built to honour the memory of all unidentified soldiers who died in the First World War.

EIFFEL TOWER

Paris, France
Construction: 2 years (1887–1889)

The Eiffel Tower is one of the world's most famous structures, a symbol of the romantic city of Paris and a proud memorial to the revolutionary spirit of France. It is also an engineering marvel that, at 300 m (984 ft) high, was the tallest structure on the planet when completed.

The tower was built for the 1889 World's Fair, which was held in Paris 100 years after the Bastille was stormed and the French Revolution began. The tower was meant to be a temporary wonder and was set to be dismantled after 20 years, but Parisians and visitors came to love its colossal beauty, and its particular usefulness as a wireless telegraph transmitter ensured its survival.

CHAMP DE MARS

The extensive green space south of the Eiffel Tower is named after Rome's Campus Martius ('Field of Mars'). The lawns here were once used as marching grounds by the French military.

Monument to the French Declaration of the Rights of Man and of the Citizen

Public garden

Before it was used by the military, the area of the Champ de Mars was a market garden. Here Parisians could grow their own fruit, vegetables and flowers.

Execution

The first mayor of Paris – Jean Sylvain Bailly – was guillotined on Champ de Mars in 1793 for giving the order to shoot the crowd during the Champ de Mars Massacre in 1791.

Pont d'Iéna

Napoleon ordered this bridge to be built in 1814 to commemorate his victory at the Battle of Jena. It is one of 37 bridges that cross the Seine in Paris.

École Militaire

This famous military school was founded in 1750. It is still an active military academy. Napoleon Bonaparte enrolled here as a 15-year-old cadet in 1784.

Wall of Peace

Erected in the year 2000, the wall has the word 'Peace' written in 49 languages on its surfaces. Visitors can place their own message of peace in the gaps in the wall.

Expositions Universelles

The Champ de Mars has hosted five World's Fairs: in 1867, 1878, 1889, 1900 and 1937.

Exposition Universelle of 1889

The tower was planned as a symbol of this World's Fair, which celebrated the centenary of the French Revolution.

Early balloon flight

One of the first-ever hydrogen-filled balloons was launched in 1783 from the spot where the tower stands today.

Isle of Swans

There was once an island in the river here, but the channel cutting it off was filled in to make the tower's setting look more symmetrical.

EIFFEL TOWER

Seine

Gustave Eiffel

Eiffel, one of the leading engineers of his time, designed railways, bridges and many notable buildings. His famous works include the Porto viaduct, Budapest railway station and the Statue of Liberty.

Sign of the times

Eiffel himself said that the tower would symbolise, 'not only the art of the modern engineer, but also the century of Industry and Science in which we are living'.

Committee of 300

The tower's design faced some fierce criticism from many people. A committee of 300 (one for every metre of the tower's height) artists, writers and architects formed to protest against it.

Guy de Maupassant

This French writer hated the tower so much that he would often eat lunch in the restaurant at its base – the one place in Paris from which he couldn't see it.

World's tallest

The tower was the world's tallest man-made structure when it was completed. It kept this title until 1930 when the Chrysler Building (318.9 m, 1,045 ft) was finished.

American inspiration

Gustave Eiffel was inspired by the Latting Observatory, which was built in New York in 1853 as part of an exhibition. At 96 m (315 ft) high, it was then the tallest structure in North America.

Ticket price

Today it costs €25 to get to the top of the tower, compared with 5 francs (€0.8) in 1889.

Rights to the tower

Gustave Eiffel's contract to build the tower granted him the rights to all income from commercial use of the monument for 20 years.

Level 3
276 m (906 ft)
The highest public observation deck in Europe.

High numbers

The tower is made up of 18,038 pieces of metal weighing 7,300 tonnes. It is held together by 2.5 million rivets. It was built by 300 workers.

Architectural sketches

5,329 drawings were made for the design of the 18,038 different parts needed in its construction.

Most visited

The Eiffel Tower is the world's most-visited paid monument, with 6,207,303 visitors in 2017.

Level 2
115 m (377 ft)
Restaurant (Michelin star)

324 m
(1,063 ft)
(tip)

Level 1
57 m (187 ft)
Restaurant
Glass floor
Audiovisual show

600 steps

You can take the stairs as far as the second level.

Solid foundations

Each leg stands on a huge limestone block set on four concrete slabs. The concrete slabs for the two legs closest to the River Seine required extra-deep piles sunk to a depth of 22 m (72 ft).

LOUVRE

Paris, France

Construction: in many stages from the 16th century to 2002

The Louvre is the largest and most-visited art museum in the world, and is home to some of the most famous artworks in history including the *Venus de Milo* and the *Mona Lisa*.

The museum is an iconic symbol of Paris and of French culture and the impressive architecture of the complex itself spans six centuries. The artistic treasures in its galleries represent cultures from prehistory to the 21st century.

The largest

The Louvre is the largest art museum in the world with a total gallery space of 72,735 m².

Fortress

The Louvre was originally built as a fortress and turned into a palace of the French Kings in 1546. In 1682 the main royal residence was moved to Versailles by Louis XIV. Some parts of the medieval Louvre castle are still visible below the ground

Location

The Louvre lies at the opposite end of the Champs-Élysées from the Arc de Triomphe.

Visitors

The museum was visited by 10.2 million people in 2018.

Nazi depot

During the German occupation of Paris in the Second World War, the Nazis used the Louvre as a store for stolen art.

Louvre pyramid

This famous pyramid made of glass and metal was built to enlarge and improve the entrance to the museum. Its incongruous modernist style and the choice of a Chinese-American architect, I.M. Pei, drew some criticism.

Paintings

The museum's collection of 7,500 paintings includes the famous works *The Raft of the Medusa, Liberty Leading the People* and the *Mona Lisa*. Around ²/₃ of the Louvre's art is by French painters.

Venus de Milo

This Greek marble sculpture from the Hellenistic period is probably the most famous classical depiction of female beauty.

Code of Hammurabi

This Babylonian code dating to 1754 BCE is one of the world's oldest examples of written law and one of the oldest readable written texts of significant length.

Exhibits

Today the museum holds 450,000 pieces of art, with around 35,000 on display in eight curatorial departments.

Louvre Abu Dhabi

In 2017, Abu Dhabi paid $525 million for the rights to use the name 'Louvre' on a new museum. The city paid a further $747 million to borrow works of art and get specialist advice from the Paris Louvre.

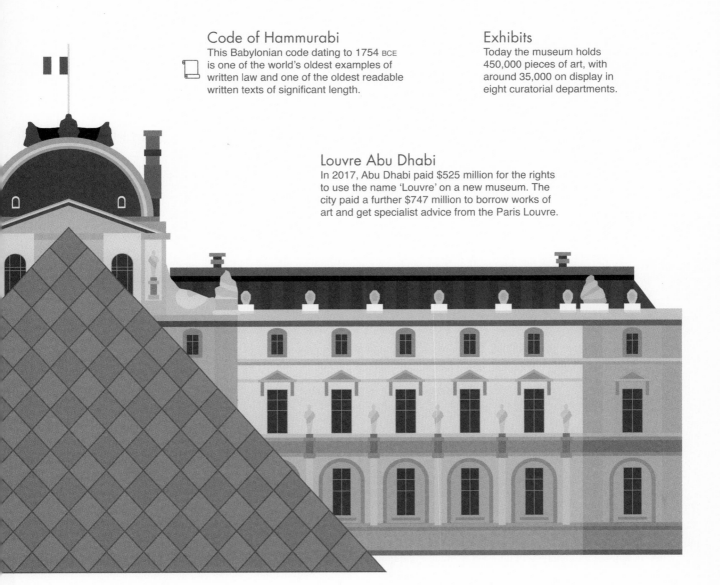

Public museum

During the French Revolution it was decided that the Louvre should be a national public museum. A small exhibition of just 537 paintings opened in 1793. The gallery space gradually expanded until it occupied almost all of the huge building.

Musée Napoleon

Napoleon renamed the museum after himself during his reign. He enlarged the collection by 5,000 pieces, largely stolen from captured cities and states. After his fall, most of the artworks were returned to the original owners.

BERLIN WALL

East Berlin, East Germany
Construction: 1961–1989 (fall of the Berlin Wall)

For 28 years the Berlin Wall stood as an infamous symbol of the Cold War, of division and of international distrust. This almost impenetrable concrete barrier was built to cut off western-controlled West Berlin from surrounding soviet-controlled East Germany and East Berlin.

Following a wave of civil unrest in soviet-controlled countries, on 9 November 1989, the East German authorities announced that travel between East and West Germany would no longer be restricted; soon after this, Berlin's 'Wall of Shame' was torn down. This ultimately led to German Reunification in 1990 and contributed to the dissolution of the Soviet Union in 1991.

Division of Germany

In 1945, during the Yalta Conference, the USA, Great Britain, France and the Soviet Union agreed to divide Germany among themselves into four occupation zones. Berlin, which was located in the middle of the Soviet zone, was also divided.

In 1949, three Western zones were unified and became democratic West Germany, while Soviet East Germany was a communist country.

Berlin

Reason for construction

From 1949 to 1961, around 2.5 million East Germans fled their part of the country to West Germany. To stop this trend, which was threatening their economy, the government of East Germany ordered the construction of a barrier between the two countries and the two parts of the city.

Length

The wall extended for 45 km (28 miles) through the middle of Berlin and another 120 km (74 miles) between West Berlin and East Germany.

Berlin Blockade

One of the first serious crises of the Cold War. During this blockade of western Berlin by the USSR in 1948–1949, deliveries of goods could only take place by air. Up to 1,400 flights a day were needed to supply the West Berlin residents.

- Berlin Wall
★ - crossings

WEST BERLIN
It occupied 54 per cent of the total area of the city. In 1987, 1.9 million people lived here. West Berlin was an enclave as it was completely surrounded by the territory of East Germany.

EAST BERLIN
It covered the major part of the historical centre of the city. In 1989, 1.3 million people lived here. East Berlin was the capital of East Germany.

Friedrichstraße station
Rail station crossing designated for foreigners.

Checkpoint Charlie
The most famous border crossing between the East and West Berlin. Meticulous control of all those crossing the border took place only on the Eastern side.

Visits

West Germans and other foreign citizens could visit East Berlin without any significant problems. It was different in the opposite direction.

"Ghost stations"

After dividing the city, some western railway lines passed without stopping through some stations on eastern territory.

Guards
At any given time, approximately 11,000 soldiers guarded the wall at the same time.

Guard dogs
Over 400 dogs guarded the wall. They ran on long leaches attached to a rail.

Fence materials
A concrete wall or wire fence with an electrified alarm.

Bunkers
Bunkers with an area of 1 m² (11 ft²) with shooting stands and ammunition stocks.

The wall
The wall was 3.6 m (11.8 ft) high and was made of reinforced concrete slabs that weighed 2.75 tons each.

Cement tube
The wall was topped with a rounded tube that made it difficult for escapees to climb up.

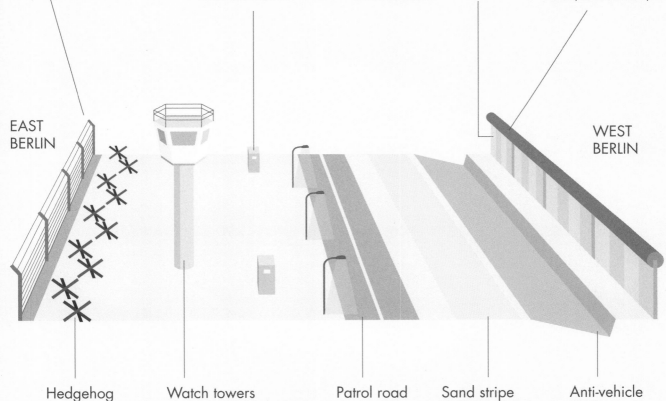

EAST BERLIN

WEST BERLIN

Hedgehog anti-vehicle obstacles

Watch towers
There were 302 watch towers at the border around West Berlin, which were Equipped with reflector and shooting stands.

Patrol road

Sand stripe
A stripe of evenly scattered sand allowed easy observation of traces of those trying to flee to the West.

Anti-vehicle ditch

Escapes
Approximately 5,000 Berliners successfully escaped through the wall and 255 were killed while trying.

Tourist attraction
On the west side of the wall there were observation towers for tourists.

ACROPOLIS OF ATHENS

Athens, Greece
Construction: 5th century BCE

For nearly 2,500 years the iconic buildings of the Acropolis have stood high on a rocky outcrop above the city of Athens. The monuments here were built by the Athenian Empire at the height of its power and influence. They are of immense architectural and historic significance and represent the crucible of Western civilisation.

The structures represent ideals of art, politics, science and faith and include the world's first theatre and earliest weather station. The Parthenon, with its elegant columns and inspired sculpture, is a symbol of Ancient Greece and is one of the world's greatest cultural monuments.

Location
The Acropolis stands on a rocky hill that rises 150 m (490 ft) above sea level and covers an area of 3 hectares (2.5 acres). The site has been used as a refuge since prehistoric times.

Erechtheion
Built between 421–406 BCE, this temple was dedicated to Athena and Poseidon (the god of the sea).

Sanctuary of Zeus Polieus
This was an open-air sanctuary dedicated to Zeus, king of all the ancient Greek gods.

Propylaea
The colossal pillared gateway to the Acropolis. Its design inspired Berlin's Brandenburg Gate.

Old Temple of Athena

Altar of Athena Polias

PARTHENON

Walls
Built over the centuries to improve defences, these stand up to 10 m (33 ft) high.

Temple of Rome and Augustus
Even though the city was conquered by Romans in 88 BCE, this is the only Roman temple on the Acropolis.

Theater of Dionysus
The world's first theatre, it was cut into a steep rocky hillside and dedicated to the god of plays and wine. The theatre could seat 17,000 people.

Tower of the Winds
This marble clocktower, located near the Acropolis, is 2,100 years old and is the world's oldest meteorological station. It had sundials, a water clock and a wind vane.

Etymology
The word acropolis comes from the Greek words akron, which means 'highest point', and polis meaning 'city'.

Damage
Athens was captured by the Ottomans in 1458. They later used the Parthenon as a gunpowder store. In 1687 during the Morean War between the Republic of Venice and the Ottoman Empire the store was hit by a cannonball. The explosion badly damaged the Parthenon and killed 300 people.

PARTHENON
In ancient Greece it served as the temple of the goddess Athena. As was customary, the temple was also used as the city treasury.

Athena
Athena was teh Ancient Greek goddess of wisdom, handicraft and warfare. She was the patron of the city Athens, which was named after her. Her symbols include owls, olive trees and snakes.

Construction
Built from 447 to 432 BCE at the peak of Greece's power.

New Gods
The Partheonon was turned into a Christian church in the the 7th century and a mosque in the 15th century.

Construction cost
At the time of construction, its cost was equivalent to building 469 warships.

Ionic order elements
The temple has some Ionic-style ornaments, including a frieze and four columns that support the roof of the inner shrine.

Columns
The Parthenon has 46 columns around its periphery. The columns are of the Doric order, the earliest and simplest of the three ancient Greek architectural orders.

Column rows
At either end of the temple there are two additional lines of six columns inside the colonnade, in front of the entrances to the interior.

Athena Parthenos
The temple housed a colossal statue of Athena made of ivory and gold. It was around 11.5 m (37 ft 9 in) high and was considered one of the greatest sculptures of ancient times. Its gold was removed in 296 BCE to pay off war debts. The statue was later lost. Some accounts mention it standing in Constantinople in the 10th century.

British removal
In the 19th century, the Parthenon was in a state of near-ruin. Many sculptures were removed by Lord Elgin and later sold to the British Government. Today they are displayed in the British Museum in London. The Greek authorities are campaigning for their return.

COLOSSEUM

Rome, Italy

Construction: 10 years (70-80 CE)

This icon of Rome was completed nearly 2,000 years ago. The largest amphitheatre in the world, it was built on a massive scale to create a suitably dramatic and capacious setting for the deadly gladiatorial combats that it hosted. The Colosseum has become the most popular tourist attraction in the world, attracting 7.4 million visitors in 2018.

Roof
Made of canvas, this was pulled out from the top level to protect viewers from rain or sun.

Name
The name 'Colosseum' probably comes from a 30-metre statue called Colossus of Nero that stood nearby. However, it was originally called the Flavian Amphitheatre, after the dynasty that built it.

New Wonder of the World
The Colosseum is listed as one of the *New7Wonders of the World*.

The largest
The Colosseum could hold between 50,000 and 80,000 people and is the largest amphitheatre ever built.

Arena
Its floor was made of wood and was covered with sand. It had an approximate size of 79 x 45 m (259 x 148 ft) and was encircled with a 4.5 m (15 ft) high wall protecting spectators from wild animals.

Elevators
Below the arena there was a series of corridors and hidden rooms from which people or animals were unexpectedly brought into battle by a system of elevators.

Unprofitability
Gladiatorial fights died out after 435 CE, probably due to the high costs of gladiator training and maintaining the venue.

Hierarchy
The five levels of seating were occupied by different social groups. The seats closest to the arena were for the emperor and senators and those furthest up for women and slaves.

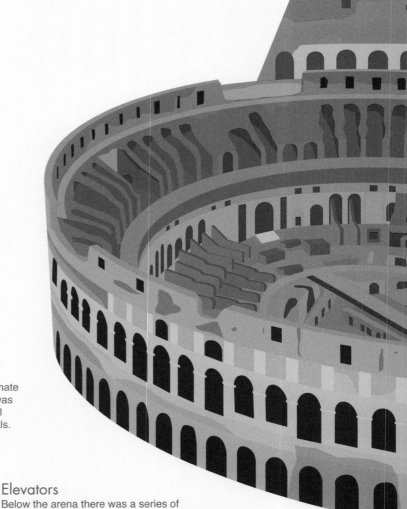

Events

 It was mostly used for gladiator battles. Over 500,000 people and millions of animals lost their lives inside its walls.

Mock sea battles

 For special occasions, the arena of the Colosseum was filled with water and naval battle scenes were enacted using miniature ships.

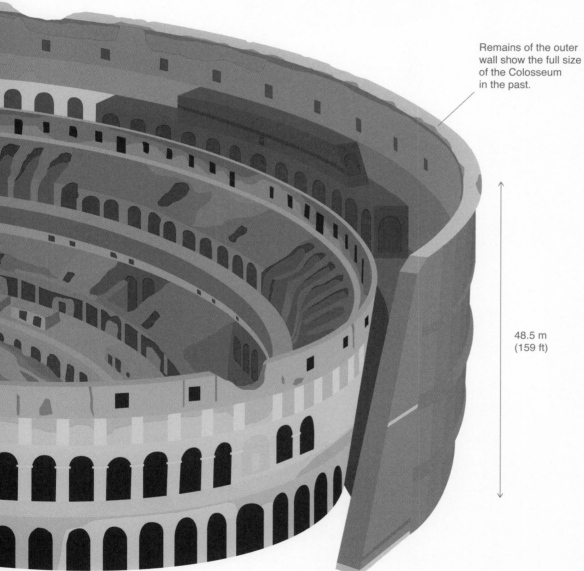

Remains of the outer wall show the full size of the Colosseum in the past.

48.5 m (159 ft)

Ruined

 The damage visible today was mostly caused by two earthquakes that hit Rome in 847 and 1231 CE.

Coins

 The building is featured on the Italian version of the 5 cent euro coin and was also depicted on ancient Roman sestertius coins.

LEANING TOWER OF PISA

Pisa, Italy
Construction: 199 years (1173–1372)

Famous for being faulty, the structure was built as the campanile (bell tower) of Pisa Cathedral. It is one of the most-photographed buildings in the world and a must-see for the 10 million tourists who visit Pisa every year.

The tower began to lean to one side soon after construction began in the 12th century. Despite many attempts to correct the tilt over the centuries, the angle increased until it reached 5.5 degrees in 1990. After a huge 8-year remediation plan was completed in 2001, the lean was reduced to 3.97 degrees and the tower has now stabilised.

Opera del Duomo
This building is now a museum that houses fine artworks, the cathedral's treasury and sacred relics. Originally, it was the residence of the cathedral's canons.

World class
UNESCO listed the 'Square of Miracles' as a World Heritage Site in 1987.

PISA TOWER

Pisa's walls
These are the oldest completely preserved walls in Italy and were completed in 1161.

Pisa Cathedral
Building of the cathedral began in 1063, the same year as St. Mark's Basilica in Venice. The rival maritime republics were each keen to show the world that they could create the most beautiful and luxurious place of worship.

Campo Santo
The name of this cemetery translates as 'holy field'. The structure is said to be built around sacred soil from Golgotha, site of the crucifixion of Jesus, brought here following a crusade in the 12th century.

Pope Gregory VIII
Gregory VIII was only pope for 57 days before he succumbed to fever in 1187. He was buried in Pisa Cathedral but his tomb was destroyed by a fire in 1600.

Baptistery of St John
The largest baptistery in Italy, this marble marvel was built on the same soft ground as the leaning tower nearby. Over the centuries it has developed a tilt of 0.6 degrees.

Piazza dei Miracoli
This serene grassy space is one of the finest architectural complexes in the world. The name 'Square of Miracles' was coined by the Italian writer and poet Gabriele d'Annunzio.

Allied bombing
In the Second World War, the Allies found out that German soldiers were using the tower as an observation post. Mindful of its beauty and historical value, they decided not to call in a bombardment.

Etymology of 'Pisa'
The exact origin of the city name is not certain, but some sources suggest it came from the Greek word meaning 'marshy land'.

Equations for a falling body
Galileo Galilei was born and studied in Pisa. Between 1589 and 1592 he used the tower in one of his celebrated experiments, dropping two cannonballs of different masses to show that their speed of descent is independent of their mass.

Pisa's towers
There are at least two other towers in Pisa that have a pronounced lean, and more than 10 in the whole of Italy.

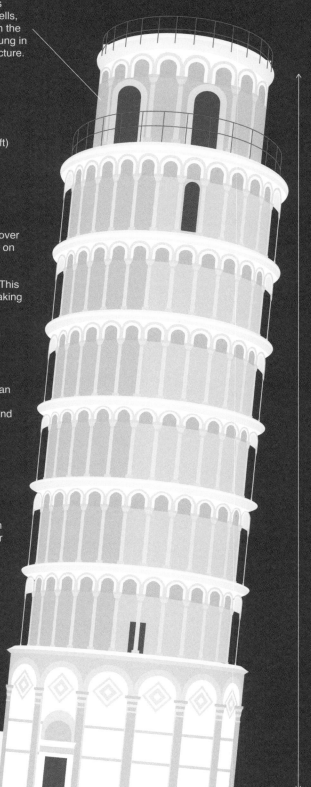

Bell-chamber
This final section of the tower was added in 1372. It houses seven bells, one corresponding to each note in the major scale. They are no longer rung in case the vibrations affect the structure.

Oversized overhang
When the tower's lean was at its greatest, a ball dropped from the top would have landed 4.5 m (15 ft) from the base.

Saving the tower
The tilting of the tower increased over the centuries until it was teetering on the brink of disaster. In 1989, the 11th-century Civic Tower in Pavia collapsed into rubble in seconds. This spurred authorities in Pisa into making plans to lessen the tower's tilt.

No pressure
The job of reducing the tower's lean and stopping it falling over was entrusted to Professor John Burland of Imperial College London, a leading expert in soil mechanics.

Engineers used a solitary drilling rig to remove earth from under the raised end of the tower one bucketful at a time.

Its tilt is now the same as it was in 1838 and should remain stable for 200–300 years.

Unknown architect
Despite the fame of the tower and its unique nature, no one knows for certain who the original designer was.

Angle
3.97 degrees

Bendy building
The tower's 3 m (10 ft) deep foundations were inadequate for the soft soil of the site. The tower began to tilt when the second floor was being built in 1178. The builders compensated for this by making the upper floors taller on one side than the other.

Weight
The tower weighs around 14,500 tonnes.

Height
On its taller side, the tower is 56.67 m (186 ft) high and has 296 steps. The opposite side is 55.86 m (183 ft) high with 294 steps.

Earthquake-proof
The tower has withstood four major earthquakes thanks to the same soft soil that led to its tilt.

Mussolini's mishap
The Italian dictator felt that the tower's crookedness was a blight on his country's honour. To straighten it he had 361 holes drilled in the foundations and injected with grout, which only served to tilt the tower even more.

AMSTERDAM OLD TOWN

Amsterdam, Netherlands
Construction: 13th century

Amsterdam grew from a tiny 13th century fishing village perched on a muddy river estuary to the wealthiest city in the western world in the 17th century. Today it is one of the world's top tourist destinations, attracting more than 5 million visitors every year. Its unique city structure – a curved lattice of peaceful canals and elegant streets – was recognised by UNESCO as a World Heritage Site in 2010. The dense old town is famous for its romantic vistas, unique architecture and lively social scene. Amsterdam is also one of the world's most multicultural cities, with inhabitants from at least 177 countries.

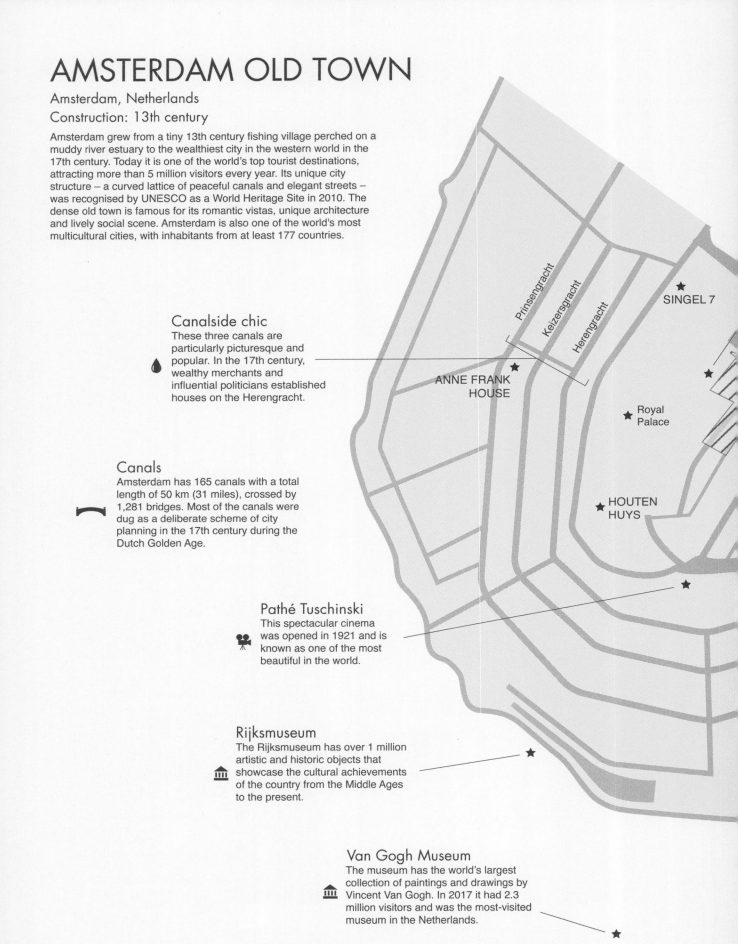

Canalside chic

These three canals are particularly picturesque and popular. In the 17th century, wealthy merchants and influential politicians established houses on the Herengracht.

Canals

Amsterdam has 165 canals with a total length of 50 km (31 miles), crossed by 1,281 bridges. Most of the canals were dug as a deliberate scheme of city planning in the 17th century during the Dutch Golden Age.

Pathé Tuschinski

This spectacular cinema was opened in 1921 and is known as one of the most beautiful in the world.

Rijksmuseum

The Rijksmuseum has over 1 million artistic and historic objects that showcase the cultural achievements of the country from the Middle Ages to the present.

Van Gogh Museum

The museum has the world's largest collection of paintings and drawings by Vincent Van Gogh. In 2017 it had 2.3 million visitors and was the most-visited museum in the Netherlands.

SINGEL 7

Prinsengracht
Keizersgracht
Herengracht

ANNE FRANK HOUSE

Royal Palace

HOUTEN HUYS

Amsterdam Stock Exchange
The oldest stock exchange in the world was established here in 1602 by the Dutch East India Company.

Red light district
In the oldest part of Amsterdam is the world's most famous red-light district.

Houseboats
There are around 2,500 houseboats in Amsterdam. Their popularity increased after many houses were destroyed by bombs during the Second World War.

Coffeeshops
There are 250 coffeeshops legally selling marijuana in Amsterdam; most of them are in the old town.

Scheepvaarthuis
The 'shipping house' is the earliest example of the 'Amsterdam School' of architecture. It was built on the spot where explorer Cornelis Houtman departed on his first trip to the East Indies in 1595.

Artis Royal Zoo
Founded in 1838, this is one of the oldest zoos in the world. It also has an aquarium and a planetarium.

DE GOOYER

MAGERE BRUG

Hortus Botanicus
One of the world's oldest botanical gardens, this was founded in 1638 by the city authorities as a herb garden to supply doctors and pharmacists with medical plants.

Amstel

Amstelsluizen
A system of locks built in 1674 allows the canals to be flushed with fresh lake water rather than tidal seawater. This innovation makes the city more pleasant to live in and is still used today.

Amstel
The city was named after this river and the dam that was built across it in the 12th century.

Clean water
The city has plans to make the water in Amsterdam's canals clean enough for people to swim in.

Crooked houses

Most of Amsterdam's houses were built on wooden piles drilled into swampy ground. As a result, many of them have shifted over the centuries and become crooked.

Piles

Today, concrete construction piles are sunk to a depth of 18 m (60 ft), much deeper than wooden piles in the past.

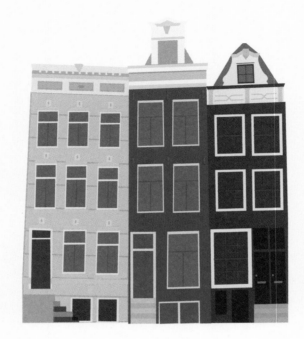

SINGEL 7

This house has the world's narrowest façade – it is just 1 m (3 ft) across.

HOUTEN HUYS

The oldest house in Amsterdam, it was built around 1420.

A rare build

Its name means 'wooden house' and today it is one of only two wooden-fronted houses in the city.

Fire risk

Construction of timber houses in Amsterdam was banned in 1521 following several disastrous fires.

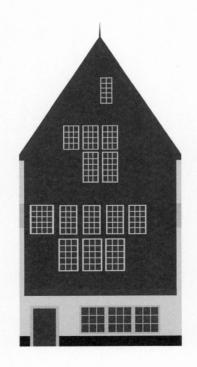

ANNE FRANK HOUSE

This is now a museum to Anne Frank, a young Jewish girl who hid here with her family and four others during the Second World War. Her famous diaries were published in 1947 and have since become the most translated Dutch book.

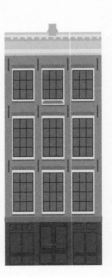

Secret annex

Anne was 13 years old when her family hid in the 46 m² (151 ft²) space at the back of the building. In 1944, they were discovered and sent to Auschwitz Birkenau concentration camp. Of the whole group, only Anne's father, Otto, survived.

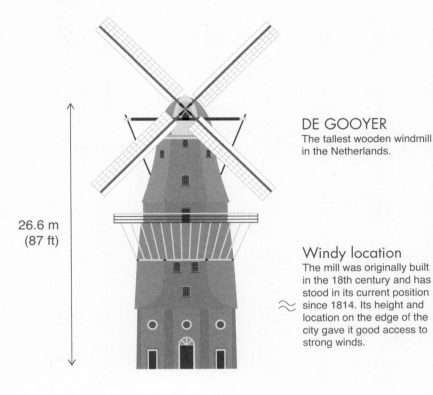

DE GOOYER
The tallest wooden windmill in the Netherlands.

26.6 m (87 ft)

Windy location
The mill was originally built in the 18th century and has stood in its current position since 1814. Its height and location on the edge of the city gave it good access to strong winds.

Bascule bridge
The bridge's central bascule section opens several times a day to allow large boats to pass through. However, local sightseeing boats are extremely low and can pass even when the bridge is closed.

MAGERE BRUG
A narrow, 13-span bridge, known as the 'Skinny Bridge', was first built here in 1691. It was replaced with a larger 9-span bridge in 1871 and by today's bascule bridge in 1934.

Two sisters
Legend says that the original bridge was built by two sisters, who lived on opposite sides of the canal and wanted to visit each other every day. However, they only had limited funds and so were forced to make the bridge very narrow.

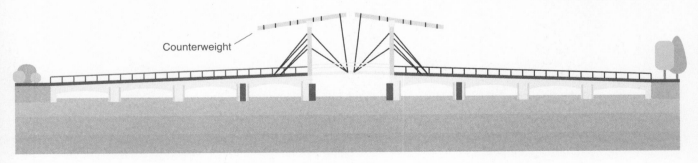

Counterweight

Bicycle graveyard
Over 10,000 bicycles are thrown away into Amsterdam's canals each year.

Ice skating
In winter, the canals often freeze solid and the city's residents enjoy skating on them.

Depth
The average depth of Amsterdam's canals is around 3 m (10 ft). A local joke says that the canals have one metre of water, one metre of mud and one metre of bicycles.

SVALBARD GLOBAL SEED VAULT

Svalbard, Norway
Construction: 2 years (2006–2008)

Nicknamed the 'doomsday seedbank', the Svalbard Global
Seed Vault was designed to survive the most severe global
cataclysms. Its mission is to preserve a wide variety of plant
seeds that represent over 10,000 years of agricultural history
since the First Agricultural Revolution, when man switched
from a lifestyle of hunting and gathering to agriculture.

Demilitarised zone
According to The Svalbard
Treaty of 1920, military
infrastructure is prohibited in
the archipelago.

Banks' bank
The Svalbard Global Seed
Vault works as a backup for
1,750 seed banks around
the world.

Drilling prohibition
Offshore petroleum drilling in
the area is prohibited by the
Norwegian government to
protect the environment.

Permafrost
The constant low temperatures of the
permafrost on the archipelago guarantee
a certain level of storage security even in
the event of a power outage.

Fauna
Animals that live around
here include Arctic foxes,
reindeer, small rodents and
polar bears.

Tectonic safety
One of the factors that
made Svalbard a
perfect location for the
vault is that it lacks
tectonic activity that
could threaten the
building.

SVALBARD
Remote, cold and
sparsely populated
archipelago that was
chosen as the perfect
location for the vault.

Arctic climate
Long, cold winters
(−16°C average
(3.2°F)) and short,
cool summers (4°C
average (39.2°F)).

Nature conservation
There are six
national parks
on the island.

No infrastructure
Since there are no roads here,
travel to the seedbank is by
snowmobile, boat or aircraft.

SVALBARD GLOBAL
SEED VAULT

First concept
Before this seedbank
was built, the Nordic
Gene Bank was storing
seeds in an abandoned
coal mine nearby.

Electricity
Provided by the nearby
power plant. Generators
guarantee energy supply in
case of a power outage.

850 km (528 miles)
to Norway.

GM free
According to Norwegian law, genetically modified seeds are prohibited here.

Funding
Entirely funded by the Norwegian government (US $8.8 million in 2008).

Unusual business trip
In 2010, seven US congressmen hand-delivered seeds of different varieties of chilli pepper.

Perpetual Repercussion
This illuminated artwork by Norwegian artist Dyveke Sanne highlights the entrance to the building from a distance. Construction projects funded by the Norwegian government that exceed a certain cost level must be decorated with artwork.

Entrance

Operational costs
All operational expenses are covered by the Crop Trust funded by multiple organisations, including the Bill & Melinda Gates Foundation. Users willing to store seeds in the vault can do so for free.

Elevation
At 130 m (426 ft) above sea level, the seedbank is well-protected from rising waters even if the ice cap melts.

Cornerstone
In 2006, the prime ministers of Denmark, Finland, Iceland, Norway and Sweden laid the vault's cornerstone.

Moat
The entrance is set over a ditch, which would prevent water from getting into the vault in the event of rising temperatures and melting snow.

SEEDS

Seeds
As of February 2018 there are 967,216 seed samples stored in the vault.

Species
There are seeds from over 5,000 plant species kept in the vault. The most popular are:
– 150,000 samples of rice
– 150,000 samples of wheat
– 80,000 samples of barley.

Packaging
Every seed sample is packed in special three-layer foil packaging. This is heat sealed to keep moisture out and then put in a plastic container.

FLOOR PLAN

Staff
The vault has no permanent staff on-site. Employees travel there for repair work or seed placement.

Low oxygen
The limited level of oxygen inside the vault slows down the metabolic processes that would age the seeds.

Floor area
Approx. 1,000 m² (10,763 ft²)

Refrigeration
The temperature inside is kept at −18°C (−0.4°F), perfect conditions for keeping seeds. If the refrigeration system failed, the temperature would rise to the bedrock's −3°C (26.6°F) in several weeks and to 0°C (32°F) in two centuries.

Storage halls
Each hall has a capacity of 1.5 million seed samples. Currently only one is in operation; the other two are empty, ready for future use.

Hall 1

Hall 2

Office

Hall 3

Entrance

150 m (492 ft)

MALBORK CASTLE

Malbork, Poland

Construction: 170 years (1280–c.1450)

This spectacular medieval fortress was founded in 1274 as the headquarters of the Teutonic Knights. The castle was expanded several times until it became the largest fortified Gothic building in Europe with 3,000 knights under its many roofs. The Teutonic Order's influence faded in the 15th century and for 300 years the castle was one of many residences of the Polish royal dynasty. Today it is the largest castle in the world and a World Heritage Site.

Name
In German it is known as the castle 'Marienburg' in honour of Mary, mother of Jesus.

Teutonic Order
The order was founded around 1190 in Acre, Kingdom of Jerusalem, to protect pilgrims travelling to the Holy Land. Its official title is 'The Order of Brothers of the German House of Saint Mary in Jerusalem'. Its knights wore white surcoats with a black cross. The order still exists today as a charitable organisation.

Palace of the Grand Masters
Architecturally this is the most impressive building in the castle complex. It contained the private rooms of the Grand Master of the Order.

Great refectory
The banquet room is the largest in the castle.

The largest
Malbork Castle is the world's largest castle by land area – 21 hectares (52 acres).

Defensive walls
Up to 6 m (20 ft) thick at their base.

Unlucky cannonball
When the castle was besieged in 1411 by Polish troops, a traitor hung a red flag outside one of the windows of a room in which a council meeting was taking place to mark a weak point in the wall. The besiegers fired an 80 kg (176 lb) cannonball in an attempt to kill the castle's commanders. It missed its target but fragments still remain in the wall today.

Sold
The castle was sold to the Polish king in 1457 for the equivalent of 660 kg (1,455 lb) of gold.

Chapel of St Anna
Burial place of 11 Great Masters of the Teutonic Order.

Destroyed
Over half of the castle was destroyed in 1945 during the German defense of the city against the Red Army. The castle is being rebuilt to this day.

Modifications
The castle has been rebuilt many times and its appearance today is probably different from the original Teutonic structure.

Chapter house
This served as a council room.

Main Tower
66 m (217 ft) tall, it served as a bell tower and a lookout point.

Dansker
This tower protruded outside the High Castle and served as both a latrine and a defensive fortification.

Unconquered
The castle has never been captured by enemy forces.

Heating system
The castle had an extensive and advanced heating system that used stoves and heat distribution channels.

High Castle

Three castles
The fortress is made up of three different castles, the High, Middle and Lower Castles. These are separated from each other by dry moats, defensive walls and towers.

Bricks
Malbork castle is the largest brick building in Europe: 12–15 million bricks were used in its construction.

Nazi destination
In the early 1930s, the castle was used by the Nazis for annual pilgrimages of the Hitler Youth.

World Heritage Site
The castle was included in the UNESCO World Heritage Site list in 1997.

MOSCOW KREMLIN

Moscow, Russia

Construction: 17th century

The Kremlin is a fortified citadel in the heart of the Russian capital that covers an area of 28 hectares (69 acres). The complex includes five palaces, four cathedrals, and is surrounded by the enclosing Kremlin Wall with its 19 imposing Kremlin towers. The complex includes the Grand Kremlin Palace, which was formerly the Moscow residence of the Tsar of Russia and is now the official residence of the President of the Russian Federation. 'Kremlin' is also used as a metonym for the Russian government.

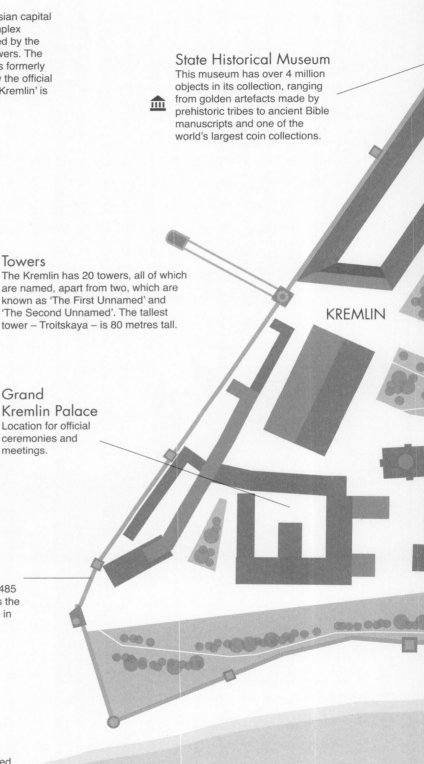

State Historical Museum
This museum has over 4 million objects in its collection, ranging from golden artefacts made by prehistoric tribes to ancient Bible manuscripts and one of the world's largest coin collections.

KREMLIN

Kremlin
The word means 'fortress inside a city'. There are many kremlins across Russia, but this is the best-known.

Towers
The Kremlin has 20 towers, all of which are named, apart from two, which are known as 'The First Unnamed' and 'The Second Unnamed'. The tallest tower – Troitskaya – is 80 metres tall.

Five stars
On top of the Kremlin, there are five stars that rotate with the wind, and each one weighs a tonne. The stars are made of ruby which makes them look very shiny and they are believed to have a 'powerful energy'.

Grand Kremlin Palace
Location for official ceremonies and meetings.

The clock tower
The Spasskaya Tower is home to the Kremlin's clock, which sits above the main entrance to Red Square. The clock's edges, hands and numbers are covered with nearly 30 kg of gold.

Kremlin Wall
Rebuilt between 1485 and 1495, this was the first brick structure in the city.

Moskva river

The city of Moscow was named after the river that runs through it.

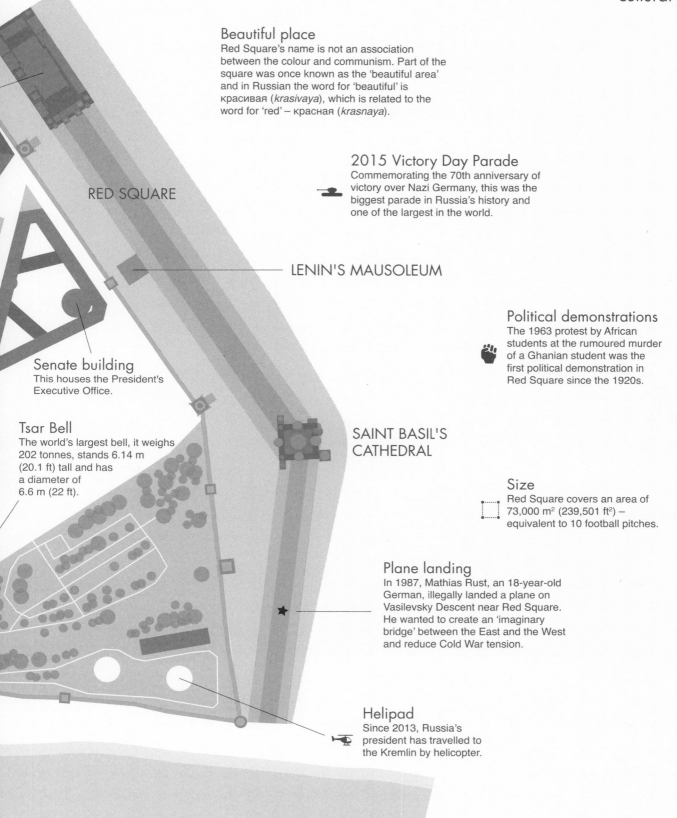

Beautiful place

Red Square's name is not an association between the colour and communism. Part of the square was once known as the 'beautiful area' and in Russian the word for 'beautiful' is красивая (*krasivaya*), which is related to the word for 'red' – красная (*krasnaya*).

2015 Victory Day Parade

Commemorating the 70th anniversary of victory over Nazi Germany, this was the biggest parade in Russia's history and one of the largest in the world.

RED SQUARE

LENIN'S MAUSOLEUM

Political demonstrations

The 1963 protest by African students at the rumoured murder of a Ghanian student was the first political demonstration in Red Square since the 1920s.

Senate building

This houses the President's Executive Office.

SAINT BASIL'S CATHEDRAL

Tsar Bell

The world's largest bell, it weighs 202 tonnes, stands 6.14 m (20.1 ft) tall and has a diameter of 6.6 m (22 ft).

Size

Red Square covers an area of 73,000 m² (239,501 ft²) – equivalent to 10 football pitches.

Plane landing

In 1987, Mathias Rust, an 18-year-old German, illegally landed a plane on Vasilevsky Descent near Red Square. He wanted to create an 'imaginary bridge' between the East and the West and reduce Cold War tension.

Helipad

Since 2013, Russia's president has travelled to the Kremlin by helicopter.

LENIN'S MAUSOLEUM

The resting place of Vladimir Lenin, head of communist Russia's government. His preserved body is on public display inside.

Vladimir Lenin

Organiser of the October Revolution of 1917, then the first leader of Soviet Russia. It is estimated that under his rule, up to 6 million people died of hunger or in prisons. He died in 1924 after suffering three strokes.

Joseph Stalin

From 1953 until 1961 Stalin's body lay next to Lenin. It was removed during reforms made by President Khrushchev.

Preservation

The mausoleum has a special team of embalmers that look after Lenin. His preserved body has to be bathed every 18 months in special chemicals. During this time, the mausoleum is closed to the public, and Lenin's clothes are carefully washed and ironed.

Suit

Lenin's body is dressed in a dark suit, and pinned to this is a Soviet Union Central Executive Committee badge.

World War II

During World War II, Lenin's body was taken to Tyumen so that it didn't get damaged. His tomb was then restored after 1945.

Opening

An initial wooden version of the tomb was opened just six days after his death. Over 100,000 people visited during the first six weeks.

Paying their respects

Over 10 million people visited Lenin's tomb between 1924 and 1972.

Pyramid

The mausoleum is a five-step pyramid made of red granite and black labradorite, and it features a 10m² mourning hall.

SAINT BASIL'S CATHEDRAL

This extraordinary multi-coloured confection of domes, spires and towers is one of Russia's most iconic symbols. It was built to commemorate Russia's victory over the Kazan Khanate in 1552.

Nine churches
The cathedral building consists of nine individual chapels, originally connected with passageways.

Colours
The cathedral's original white paint was replaced with vivid colours from the 17th–19th centuries.

Church of the Intercession
The largest of cathedral's chapels has a floor area of only 64 m².

Onion domes
Originally gold, these were probably added to the newly-rebuilt church after it burned down in 1583.

Flame design
Its shape was designed to resemble a bonfire leaping skywards, and its design is unique to Russian architecture.

Original bell
Only one of the original bells survived the 1929 Soviet order to melt down all the bronze bells.

Museum
Today, the church is a museum.

Survival
The cathedral miraculously survived Napoleon's 1812 invasion and Stalin's plan to destroy all religious buildings.

Height
47.5 m (156 ft). Until 1600 it was the tallest building in Moscow.

Ivan the Terrible
Built by order of the tsar who transformed Russia into an empire. He was known for his cruelty and mental instability.

Blinded architects
A myth says that Ivan the Terrible blinded the cathedral's architect so he could never build anything as beautiful again.

Secularisation
In 1923, the church was confiscated by the anti-theist Soviet government. It is still owned by the state, although weekly religious services have been held since 1997.

TRANS-SIBERIAN RAILWAY

Russia

Construction: 25 years (1891–1916)

From the heart of the largest city in Europe to the shores of the Pacific Ocean, across one of the world's great wildernesses and along Earth's mightiest lake, the Trans-Siberian Railway is a journey unlike any other.

The railway itself is also a formidable technical achievement. Engineers had to tame the permafrost of Siberia and bridge hundreds of rivers to build the world's longest railway.

Travel time
The train takes eight days to complete the route. It would take about five days non-stop to drive this distance by car and around 73 days to walk it.

The longest
Stretching for 9,289 km (5,772 miles) it is the world's longest railway. That's roughly the same distance between London and Rio de Janeiro.

Time zones
The railway goes through eight different time zones.

Industrialisation
The railway was built to connect the Russian Far East with the more developed European region of the country and to boost its industrialisation.

Yaroslavl

Moscow
At the western end, the Trans-Siberian trains leave Moscow from Yaroslavsky station, the busiest of the capital's railway stations.

Kirov

Perm

Ekaterinburg

Tyumen

Krasnoyarsk

Omsk

Novosibirsk
With 1.6 million residents, this is the most populous city in Siberia.

Tsar project
Construction of the railway began during the reign of Tsar Alexander III (1881–1894) and it was completed during the reign of Tsar Nicholas II (1894–1917).

World War II
Until the German attack on the Soviet Union in 1941, the railway was used to transport goods between the Axis powers and their ally, Japan.

Train ferries
These were proposed as cheaper alternatives to building bridges on some river crossings.

Construction
The design of the railway was divided into seven sections, which were all built independently.

Workers
Around 62,000 people worked on the construction of the railway, mostly soldiers and convicts.

Tickets
The cheapest tickets for the trip start at €150.

Electric locomotives
Electrification of the railway started in 1929.

Siberia
This region is known for its harsh winters and, historically, for its labour camps, and is one of the world's most sparsely populated areas. It covers 77 per cent of the country but has only 27 per cent of Russia's population.

Lake Baikal
The world's deepest and largest freshwater lake by volume. It contains 22–23 per cent of the planet's fresh surface water.

Skovrodino

Belogorsk

Khabarovsk
The bridge over the Amur river here was the last piece of the railway to be completed.

Tayshet

Chita

Ulan-Ude

Irkutsk
Trains first reached this city in 1898.

Vladivostok
The only ice-free large port in the Russian Far East and the headquarters of the Russian Pacific Fleet.

Russo-Japanese War
During this war (1904–1905) the Trans-Siberian Railway was used to transport soldiers to the war zone. But its single track limited capacity and contributed to Russia's defeat.

Cargo shipment
The Trans-Siberian Railway is a faster way to transport goods from China compared to the sea journey of a month. The railway carries 200,000 containers to Europe every year.

CAMP NOU

Barcelona, Spain
Construction: 3 years (1954–1957)

This huge, three-tiered stadium has been intimidating FC Barcelona's opponents for over 60 years. It is the largest football stadium in Europe and a world-famous landmark of Barcelona. It's a fitting home for the club that domestically has won a record 74 trophies: 26 La Liga, 30 Copa del Rey, 13 Supercopa de España, three Copa Eva Duarte, and two Copa de la Liga trophies.

Scoreboards
The first electronic version was installed in 1975.

The third tier of seating was added for the 1982 World Cup.

The largest
With a capacity of 99,354, this is the largest football stadium in Europe and the third-largest in the world.

Safety first
Despite Camp Nou's size and capacity, it can be evacuated in only 5 minutes – making it one of the safest stadiums in the world.

FC Barcelona
Barcelona are the world's fourth-most valuable sports team (valued at $4 billion). They have never been relegated from the highest Spanish division.

Highest attendance
When the stadium first opened it could accommodate 106,146 people. Its record attendance is 120,000 spectators, at the 1986 European Cup quarter-final against Juventus.

Club museum
Opened in 1984, it had 1.8 million visitors in 2015 and is one of the most visited museums in Spain.

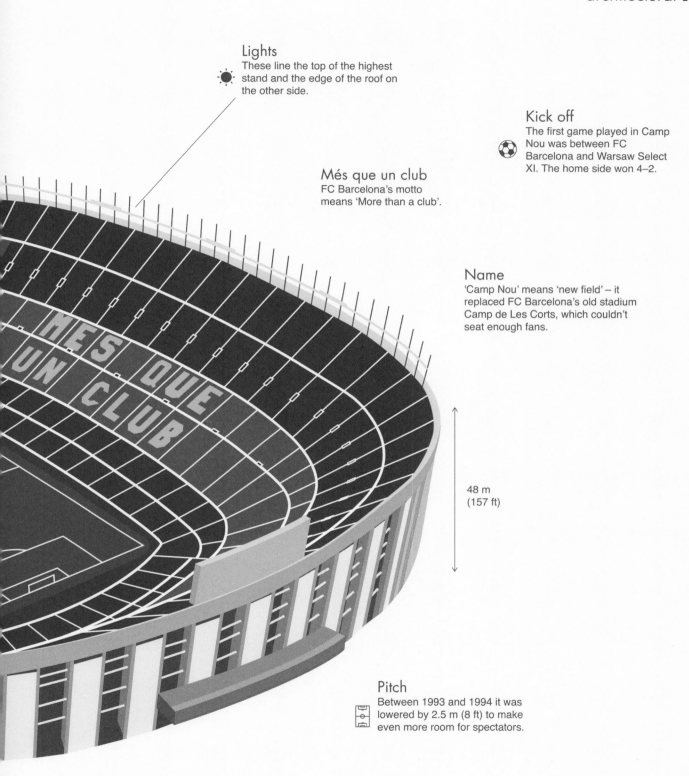

Lights
These line the top of the highest stand and the edge of the roof on the other side.

Kick off
The first game played in Camp Nou was between FC Barcelona and Warsaw Select XI. The home side won 4–2.

Més que un club
FC Barcelona's motto means 'More than a club'.

Name
'Camp Nou' means 'new field' – it replaced FC Barcelona's old stadium Camp de Les Corts, which couldn't seat enough fans.

MÉS QUE
UN CLUB

48 m
(157 ft)

Pitch
Between 1993 and 1994 it was lowered by 2.5 m (8 ft) to make even more room for spectators.

Pope's visit
In 1982, Pope John Paul II celebrated mass here for more than 121,500 people.

Expansion
By 2021, at a cost of around €600 million, the stadium will be expanded to a capacity of 105,000 and all the stands will be covered by a roof.

GUGGENHEIM MUSEUM BILBAO

Bilbao, Spain
Construction: 4 years (1993–1997)

One of the world's most spectacular buildings, this museum provides a fitting home for an outstanding collection of modern and contemporary art. The museum helped revitalise a decaying former port area and has become a major cultural hub for the Basque region.

Designer
The museum was designed by Frank Gehry, a star among contemporary American architects. He was specifically asked to create a daring and innovative building; the result is one of his most recognised works.

"Snake"
This 100 m long, 180 tonnes metal sculpture is amongst the most famous works exhibited in the museum.

Tower

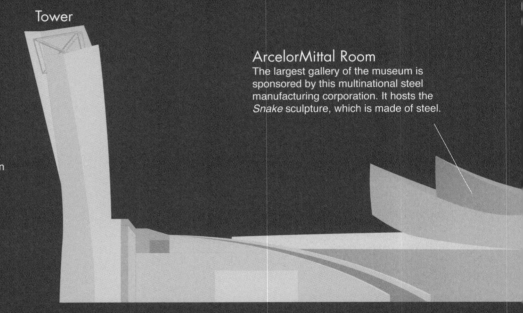

ArcelorMittal Room
The largest gallery of the museum is sponsored by this multinational steel manufacturing corporation. It hosts the *Snake* sculpture, which is made of steel.

Space to spare
When the museum opened it had more exhibition space than the three other Guggenheim museums combined.

Guggenheim Museums
There are currently four museums established by the Solomon R. Guggenheim Foundation. They are in New York City, Venice, Bilbao and Abu Dhabi (under construction).

Area
The museum has a total floor area of 46,000 m².

Titanium
Some curved metal walls are made from titanium only 0.5 mm thick.

Naval inspiration
The shape of the building echoes a sailing ship, in a reference to the dockside location and naval character of the city.

Visitors
The museum was visited by 1.3 million people in 2018.

Project funding

The Basque Government covered the construction costs, created a $ $50 million acquisitions fund and subsidises the museum's $12 million annual budget.

Construction cost

$89 million

Opening

The museum was opened by King Juan Carlos I of Spain in 1997.

Skylights

The building has many large but hidden skylights that allow light to softly filter down to the interior.

Fraud

In 2007, a scandal broke: large sums of money had been stolen from the museum's accounts and were found in the director's private account.

Irregular rooms

Irregular shapes of galleries inside the museum conform to the design of its exterior.

Limestone

The straight walls are built from limestone.

Galleries

There are 20 galleries, designed in a variety of shapes to change the perspective of the viewer.

Load-bearing walls

The construction focuses on load-bearing walls and ceilings. This approach has created large gallery spaces inside the building that are not cluttered up by interior supporting columns.

Promotion

The project was part of the revitalisation plan for Bilbao. It significantly raised global awareness of a previously little-known city and attracted millions of tourists, who generated approx. €500 million in economic activity in the region within three years of the museum's opening.

Virtual design

The complex design was constructed on time and budget partly thanks to pioneering virtual modelling processes that set a benchmark for the use of computer visualisations in architecture.

PALACE OF WESTMINSTER & WESTMINSTER ABBEY

London, England

Construction: Palace of Westminster – 36 years (1840–1876),
Westminster Abbey – 680 years (1065–1745)

Thanks to its striking Gothic Revival architecture, huge scale and unique location on the River Thames, The Palace of Westminster is one of the world's best-known buildings. It holds the meeting chambers of both the House of Commons and the House of Lords and is usually referred to as the Houses of Parliament. With its famous clock tower and Big Ben bell, it is a commonly used symbol of London and indeed Britain.

Westminster Abbey is one of the United Kingdom's best-known religious buildings and is the customary place of coronation for English and British monarchs. There have been 16 royal weddings in the Abbey and it is the resting place of many notable people, including 16 monarchs and eight Prime Ministers.

Westminster tube station
This busy station handled 25.6 million passengers in 2017. When the Jubilee line was extended through the station in 1999, a 39 m (128 ft) deep hole was dug beneath the old station to accommodate the new platforms – the deepest ever excavation in central London.

St. Margaret's Church
This church was built in the grounds of Westminster Abbey in the 12th century so that local people could have a simpler parish church to worship in. In 1987 it was included with the Palace of Westminster and Westminster Abbey on the UNESCO World Heritage List.

BIG BEN

The Supreme Court

Parliament Square Garden

PALACE OF WESTMINSTER

WESTMINSTER ABBEY

Westminster Bridge
The bridge is painted green, the same colour as the seats in the House of Commons. Lambeth Bridge, on the opposite side of the Houses of Parliament, is painted red, the same colour as the seats in the House of Lords.

Old Palace
In 1834, a stove used to burn wooden tally sticks started a fire that destroyed the Old Palace.

Statue of George V
During his reign (1910–1936) the British Empire became the largest in history, covering 24 per cent of all land on Earth and ruling 458 million people – ¼ of the world's population.

River Thames
Around 70 per cent of London's drinking water comes from the river. It is collected into reservoirs to the west of London, before the river reaches the city.

Jewel Tower
Built in the 13th century, for 300 years this was used to store the monarch's personal treasure.

College Green
With the Houses of Parliament forming a dramatic backdrop, this is a popular location for TV interviews and reports.

WESTMINSTER ABBEY
The coronation and burial site for British monarchs.

Flag
The flag flying here is chosen, depending on the occasion, from several options: the Commonwealth Nations Flag, the Flag of St Peter, the Abbey Flag, the Union Flag, the Flags of the National Saints, the Royal Air Force Flag, and the Royal Standard.

William the Conqueror
He was the first monarch to be crowned here, in 1066. Since then, all English and UK monarchs except Edward V and Edward VIII have been crowned here.

Queen Elizabeth II
Her coronation in 1953 was the first to be broadcast on television.

69 m
(226 ft)

Burials
Over 3,300 people have been laid to rest in the Abbey, including 17 monarchs, and famous people such as Issac Newton and Charles Dickens.

Jerusalem Chamber
This spectacular room was once part of the abbot's house of Westminster Abbey. King Henry IV died here in front of the fireplace in 1413.

PALACE OF WESTMINSTER

Commonly named the Houses of Parliament.
Designed in English Gothic architectural style.

In 1834, a savage fire ripped through the medieval
buildings that made up the Houses of Parliament. A
competition held in 1836 for the reconstruction of the
Palace was won by the architect Charles Barry. The
New Palace is much larger than the old complex, with
an area of 3.2 hectares (8 acres), over 1,100 rooms
and an impressive 300 m long (980 ft) façade built
on land newly reclaimed from the River Thames. The
few remains of the Old Palace (except the detached
Jewel Tower) were incorporated into the new
replacement.

Augustus Pugin
Although it was Charles Barry that won
the contract for the construction of the
palace, he relied heavily on Augustus
Pugin's input. Pugin designed much of
the palace's interior – from the panelling
and carving to the doorknobs.

Victoria Tower
This stores over 3 million parliamentary
records on 9.6 km (6 miles) of shelving across
12 floors. Some records date back to 1497.
The tower is 98.5 m (323 ft) tall – 2.2 m (7 ft)
taller than the more famous Elizabeth Tower
at the north end of the Palace.

Roof
There are around 8,000
tiles on the roof, each
weighing 75 kg (165 lb).

House of Lords chamber
This is the most ornate room in the
Palace and the meeting place of the
upper house of the Parliament of the
United Kingdom. It has only around
400 seats for the 792 members who
are eligible to sit in the chamber.

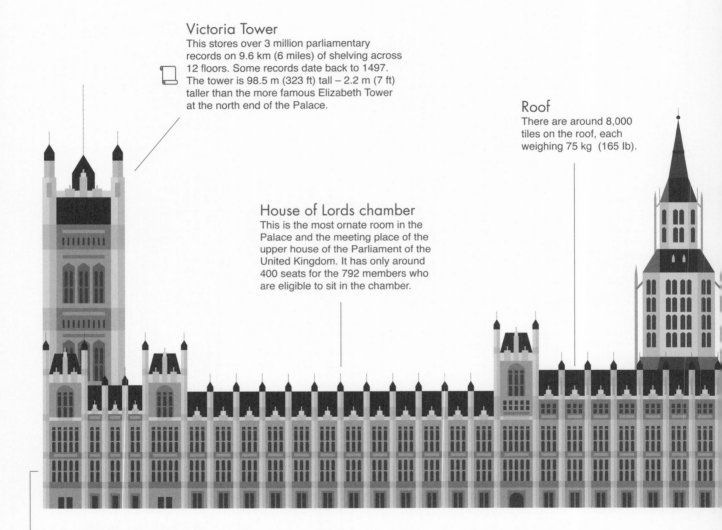

Principal floor
The Palace's main rooms
are on the first floor.

Windows
There are around 3,400
stained glass windows.

Big Ben

Technically this is the name of the largest of the five bells in the tower, although it is often used to refer to the tower. Officially this was named Elizabeth Tower in 2012 to mark the Diamond Jubilee of Elizabeth II. Its clock is cleaned every five years. If you stand at the base of this tower, you'll hear the bell ringing later than a person who listens to it in a live transmission on the other side of the country.

Refurbishment

In 2018, MPs voted for major refurbishment of the Palace of Westminster to take place. The works are estimated to cost around £3.5 billion and will mean that MPs have to relocate for 6 years while the work is completed.

Ayrton Light

This is lit when either of the Houses of Parliament is sitting. It was added in 1885 so that Queen Victoria could see it from Buckingham Palace.

House of Commons chamber

The meeting place of the lower house of the Parliament of the United Kingdom. It has only 427 seats for 650 members. Traditionally the British monarch does not enter this chamber.

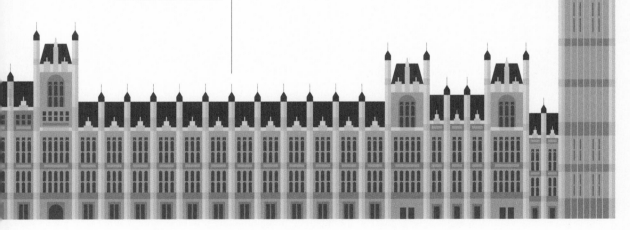

96 m
(315 ft)

Stone conservation

Restoring the stone exterior took 13 years, from 1981 to 1994.

Size

The Palace has over 1,100 rooms and 4.8 km (2.9 miles) of passageways.

STONEHENGE

Wiltshire, England

Construction: 1c.1,500 years (3100–1600 BCE)

Stonehenge is the most architecturally advanced prehistoric stone circle in the world and a unique record of our ancient heritage. The first henge structures here were built 5,000 years ago.

The great stone circle was constructed around 2500 BCE – about the same time as the Great Pyramid of Giza. Burial mounds and circles of smaller stone were added later. This instantly recognisable monument lies at the heart of a wider area that is incredibly rich in archaeological treasures. There are many proposed theories as to who built Stonehenge and for what purpose.

Closed road
The busy A344 road passed only 50 m (164 ft) from the monument. In 2013 it was closed and demolished because traffic vibrations threatened the monument.

World Heritage Site
It was added onto UNESCO's heritage list in 1986.

Burial ground
Stonehenge was probably built as a burial ground; several hundred burial mounds have been found.

Merlin myth
A 12th-century myth says that Merlin brought magical stones from Mount Killaraus in Ireland and built Stonehenge as a memorial to dead princes.

Sold
In 1915, a local businessman bought Stonehenge at auction for £6,600 as a gift to his wife. Three years later he gave it to the nation.

Slaughter stone
Its reddish patches have been associated with the blood of victims sacrificed by the Druids. In fact, iron in the stone causes the colour.

Limited visits
Since 1978, access to the centre of the ring has been strictly limited to protect the stones.

First excavations
These were carried out in 1620 on behalf of the Duke of Buckingham.

HEEL STONE

TRIPLE TRILITHON

ALTAR STONE

STONE 56

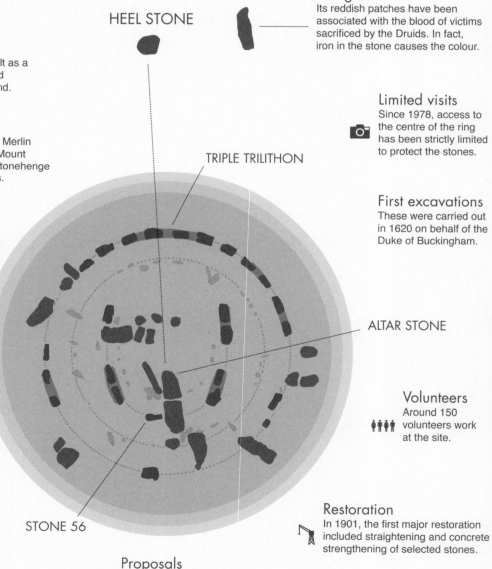

- sarsen stone
- blue stone

Sarsen stones
These weigh 25 tonnes on average. The Heel Stone is the biggest sarsen stone at 30 tonnes.

Blue stones
These 1–2 tonne stones were brought from South Wales over 240 km (150 miles) away, probably by boat.

Proposals
Every month 1–2 people pop the question here.

Volunteers
Around 150 volunteers work at the site.

Restoration
In 1901, the first major restoration included straightening and concrete strengthening of selected stones.

Great Trilithon

There were once five trilithons inside the circle, each with two uprights and a lintel. These huge stones weighed up to 50 tonnes each.

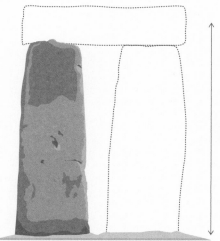

8.71 m
(28.5 ft)

STONE 56

One upright from the Great Trilithon stands today. It's the tallest stone at the site, with 6.7 m (22 ft) visible and 2.4 m (7.9 ft) underground.

HEEL STONE

The stone weighs about 35 tonnes and lies 77.4 m outside the centre of the circle.

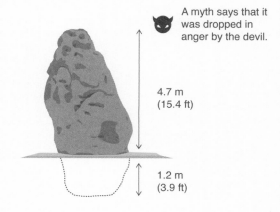

A myth says that it was dropped in anger by the devil.

4.7 m
(15.4 ft)

1.2 m
(3.9 ft)

ALTAR STONE

A central megalith that may have served as the altar.

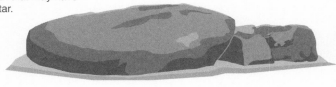

Cracked

It was broken into two pieces by the fall of the Great Trilithon's upright.

TRIPLE TRILITHON

Naturally preserved, it did not require reconstruction. Its three lintel sections used to be part of a circle of 30 trilithons surrounding the centre of the monument.

Lintels

Each of these three lintels weighs 4.5–6.5 tonnes, around the same as the heaviest land mammal – an African Elephant.

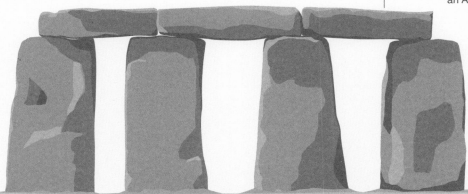

VATICAN CITY

Italian Peninsula, Europe
Construction: started in 1st century CE

The Vatican City is an independent city state that sits within Rome, the capital city of Italy. Within the walls of the Vatican City, there are many well-known religious and cultural sites, for example, St Peter's Basilica and the Vatican Museums, which are home to some of the world's most famous pieces of art.

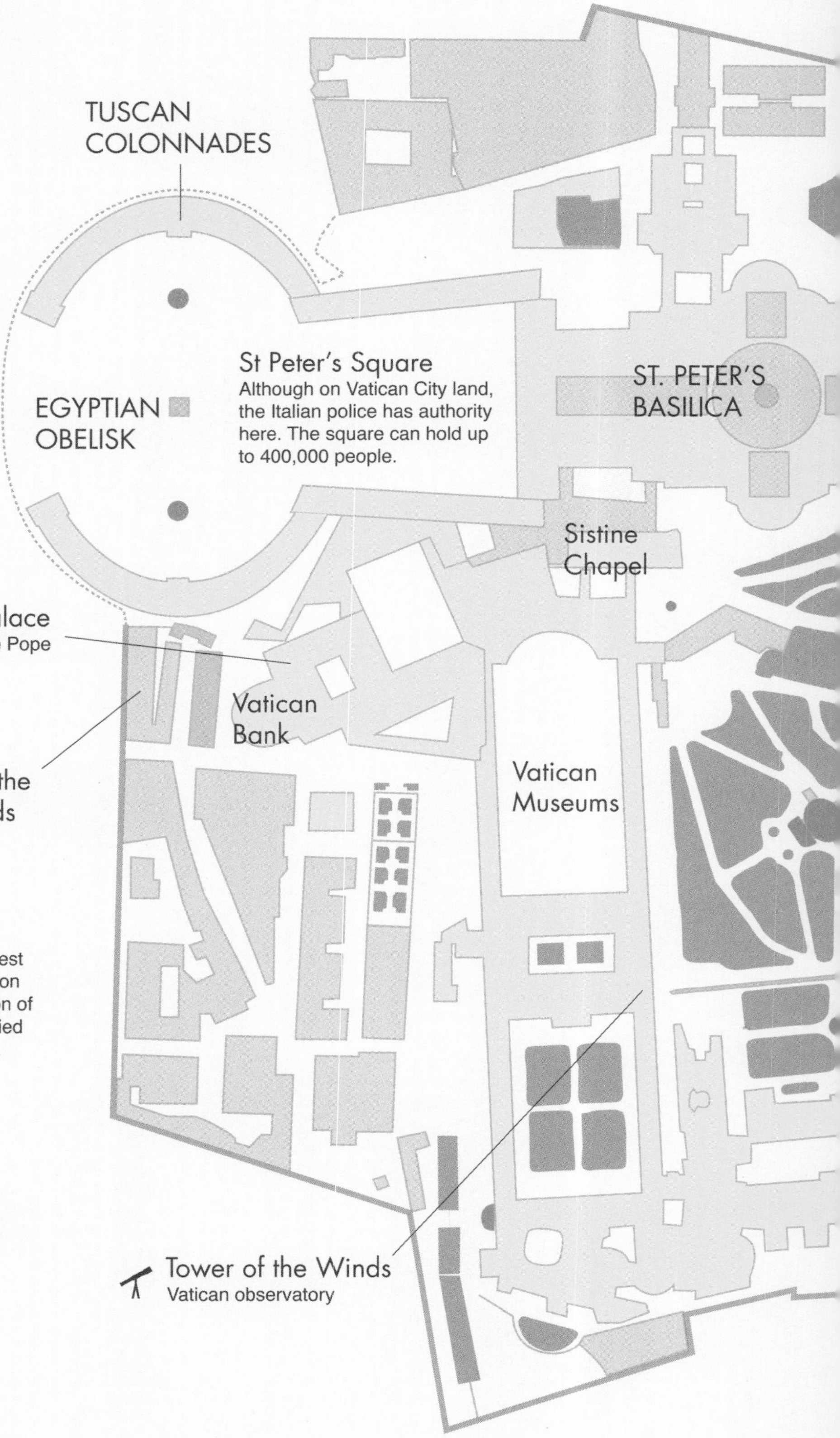

TUSCAN COLONNADES

Saint Peter
The Square and Basilica are named after Saint Peter, one of Christ's Twelve Apostles, and the first Pope.

EGYPTIAN OBELISK

St Peter's Square
Although on Vatican City land, the Italian police has authority here. The square can hold up to 400,000 people.

ST. PETER'S BASILICA

Sistine Chapel

Apostolic Palace
Residence of the Pope

Vatican Bank

Barracks of the Swiss Guards

Vatican Museums

Swiss Guard
Established in 1506, this is the oldest military force in continuous operation and is responsible for the protection of the Pope. Guards must be unmarried Swiss Catholic males aged 19–30.

Sistine Chapel
The papal conclave, the meeting of cardinals to elect the new pope, takes place here.

Tower of the Winds
Vatican observatory

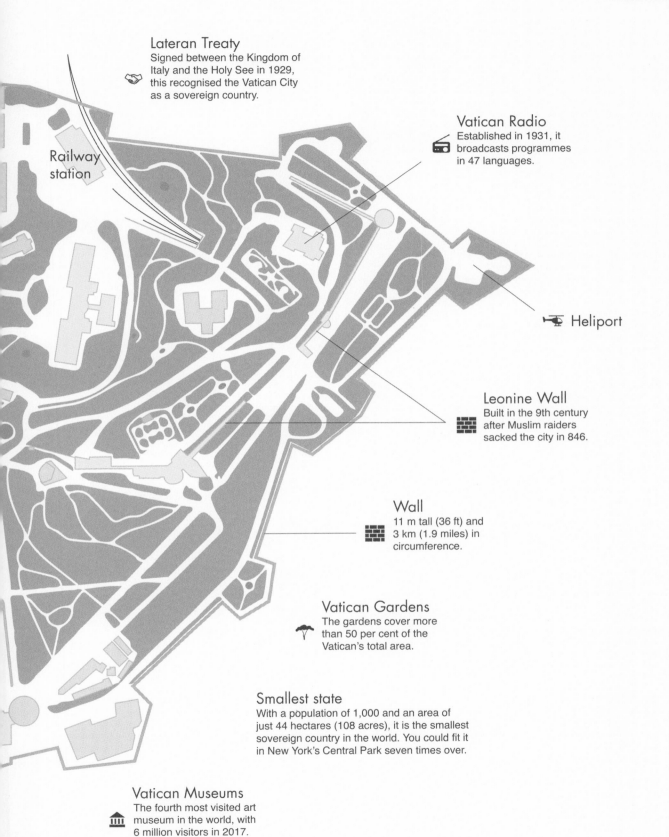

Lateran Treaty
Signed between the Kingdom of Italy and the Holy See in 1929, this recognised the Vatican City as a sovereign country.

Railway station

Vatican Radio
Established in 1931, it broadcasts programmes in 47 languages.

Heliport

Leonine Wall
Built in the 9th century after Muslim raiders sacked the city in 846.

Wall
11 m tall (36 ft) and 3 km (1.9 miles) in circumference.

Vatican Gardens
The gardens cover more than 50 per cent of the Vatican's total area.

Smallest state
With a population of 1,000 and an area of just 44 hectares (108 acres), it is the smallest sovereign country in the world. You could fit it in New York's Central Park seven times over.

Vatican Museums
The fourth most visited art museum in the world, with 6 million visitors in 2017.

In the Middle Ages it was thought that Julius Caesar's ashes were hidden in the gilt ball on top of the Obelisk.

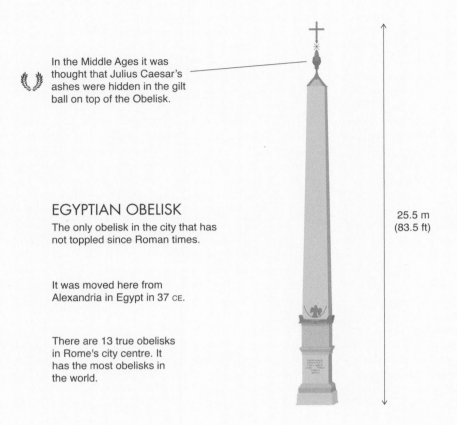

EGYPTIAN OBELISK

The only obelisk in the city that has not toppled since Roman times.

It was moved here from Alexandria in Egypt in 37 CE.

There are 13 true obelisks in Rome's city centre. It has the most obelisks in the world.

25.5 m (83.5 ft)

TUSCAN COLONNADES

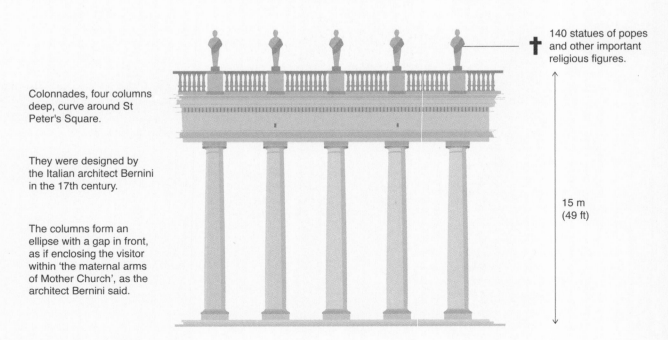

140 statues of popes and other important religious figures.

Colonnades, four columns deep, curve around St Peter's Square.

They were designed by the Italian architect Bernini in the 17th century.

The columns form an ellipse with a gap in front, as if enclosing the visitor within 'the maternal arms of Mother Church', as the architect Bernini said.

15 m (49 ft)

ST PETER'S BASILICA
The largest church in the world by
interior area – 15,160 m² (163,181 ft²)

Unethical financing
$ The construction was financed to a large extent
by the granting of indulgences (a reduction in
the punishment for a sin for money).

Not a cathedral
The Basilica is not the seat of a bishop
and so is therefore not a cathedral. It is
still one of the holiest of Catholic shrines.

Architects
Eight architects
contributed to
the design.

The world's tallest
dome and the
second-tallest
building in Rome.

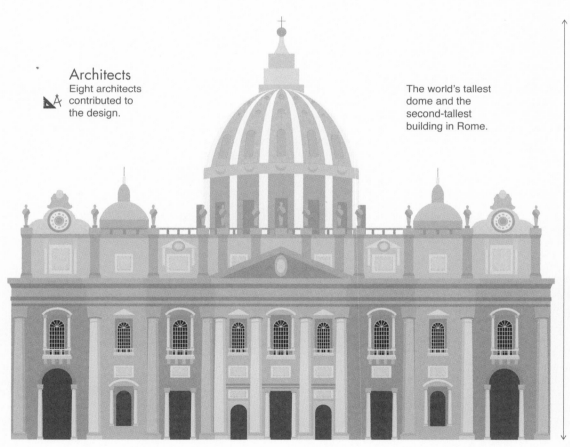

136.6 m
(448 ft)

Saint Peter's death
Christian tradition says that Saint Peter
was inversely crucified in the place
where the basilica stands today. He is
buried directly beneath the high altar.

Tombs
St Peter's Basilica holds
over 100 tombs, including
the bodies of 91 popes.

Michelangelo
One of the greatest artists of all time,
Michelangelo was the principal designer
of the Basilica. However, he was forced
to take the job by the Pope when other
candidates either refused or died.

The Bibliotheca
Alexandrina was the site
of the first external backup
of the Internet Archive.

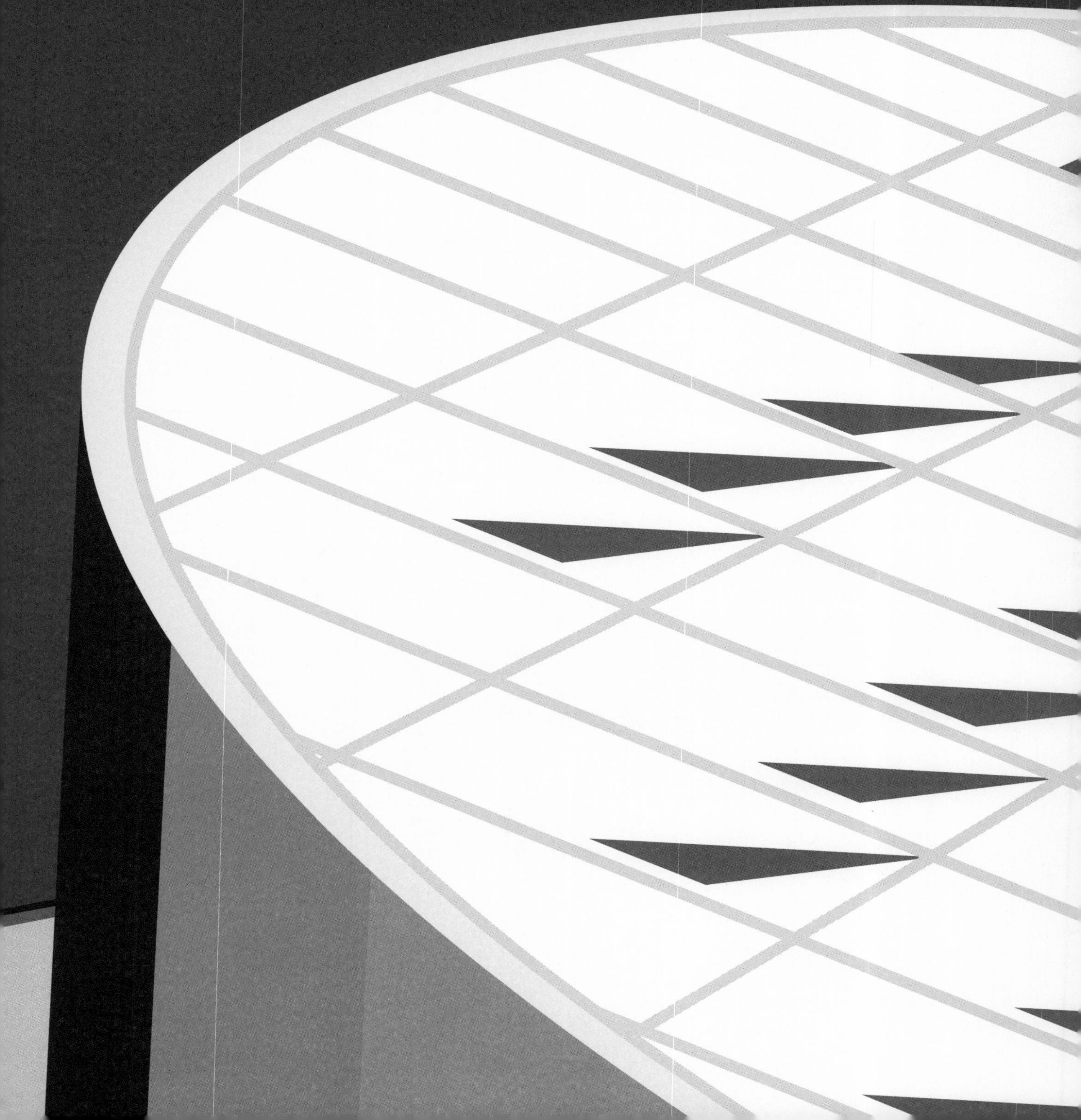

Africa

GREAT PYRAMIDS

Giza, Egypt

Construction: 70 years (2580–2510 BCE)

The Great Pyramids in Giza, Egypt, are the biggest and oldest pyramids in Egypt. The pyramids were built as tombs for pharaohs and took around 20 years to construct. Around 10 million tourists visit the site every year.

How many?
There are 118 pyramids in Egypt.

Cairo city centre – 13 km (8 miles)

Pointing north
The sides of the Giza pyramids are almost perfectly oriented towards the four cardinal compass directions.

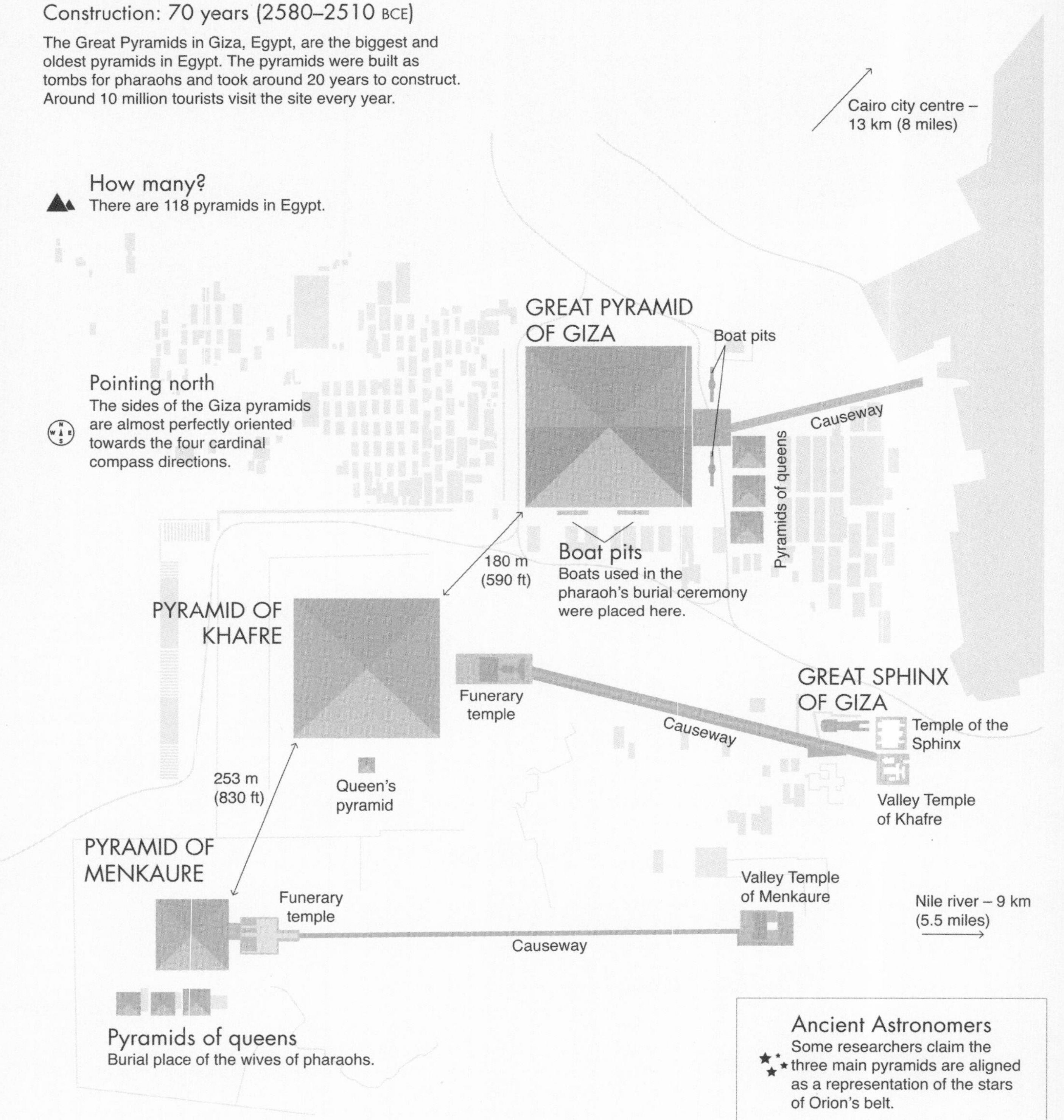

GREAT PYRAMID OF GIZA

Boat pits

Causeway

Pyramids of queens

Boat pits
Boats used in the pharaoh's burial ceremony were placed here.

180 m (590 ft)

PYRAMID OF KHAFRE

253 m (830 ft)

Queen's pyramid

Funerary temple

Causeway

GREAT SPHINX OF GIZA

Temple of the Sphinx

Valley Temple of Khafre

PYRAMID OF MENKAURE

Funerary temple

Causeway

Valley Temple of Menkaure

Nile river – 9 km (5.5 miles)

Pyramids of queens
Burial place of the wives of pharaohs.

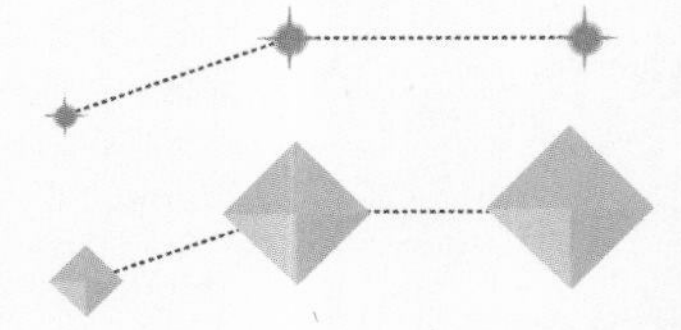

Demolition
In the 12th century, the son of Saladin planned to demolish the pyramids but the cost would have been almost as high as building them.

Sunset
Pyramids were built on the River Nile's west bank – the side of the setting sun, which was a symbol of the realm of the dead in Egyptian mythology.

Ancient Astronomers
Some researchers claim the three main pyramids are aligned as a representation of the stars of Orion's belt.

GREAT PYRAMID OF GIZA
The largest and oldest of the Giza pyramids, this is the tomb of Pharaoh Khufu, who ruled Egypt from 2589 to 2566 BCE.

Tallest building
At 146.7 m (481 ft) it was the world's tallest man-made structure for 3,800 years until 1311 when Lincoln Cathedral (160 m, 525 ft) was completed. Today it is only 138.8 m (455 ft) tall.

Huge mass
Its mass is estimated at 5.9 million tonnes, nearly 2 million tonnes heavier than the world's heaviest building, the Palace of the Parliament in Bucharest.

Stolen limestone
The Great Pyramid was once covered with polished white limestone, which was stolen in 1356 for the construction of a mosque and fortress.

Supposedly air shafts

Mysterious, large and inaccessible cavity, discovered in 2017 with the use of Muon tomography.

138.8 m (455.3 ft). Originally 146.7 m (481.2 ft)

Grand Gallery
8.6 m (28.2 ft)

King's Chamber

Queen's Chamber

Entrance

Unfinished chamber of unknown purpose

Seven Wonders
The oldest of the Seven Wonders of the Ancient World and the only one that stands today.

US$5 billion
The estimated cost of building the Great Pyramid today.

Workers
It took an average workforce of about 14,500 people and a peak workforce of roughly 40,000 over 20 years to build the Great Pyramid.

Leveled base
Construction required a level foundation achieved by surrounding the site with walls, filling the enclosed space with water and repeatedly draining the water to lower protruding land.

Water cuts stone
Large stones used for construction were split by inserting pieces of wood into small drilled holes and soaking them in water. As they expanded, they cracked the stone.

85

PYRAMID OF MENKAURE

The pyramid of Menkaure is probably the tomb of the son of the Pharaoh Khafre.

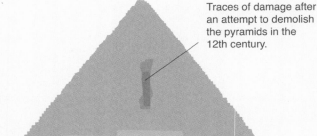

Lost sarcophagus

A beautiful sarcophagus found in the Pyramid of Menkaure was lost off the coast of Spain in 1838 when the ship taking it to Britain sank.

Traces of damage after an attempt to demolish the pyramids in the 12th century.

At 61 m (200 ft) tall, it is the smallest of Giza's three major pyramids.

PYRAMID OF KHAFRE

The pyramid of Khafre is the tomb of the pharaoh Khafre, who ruled Egypt over 4,500 years ago.

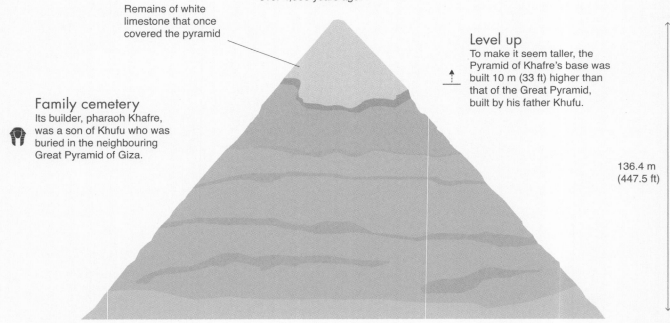

Remains of white limestone that once covered the pyramid

Level up

To make it seem taller, the Pyramid of Khafre's base was built 10 m (33 ft) higher than that of the Great Pyramid, built by his father Khufu.

Family cemetery

Its builder, pharaoh Khafre, was a son of Khufu who was buried in the neighbouring Great Pyramid of Giza.

136.4 m (447.5 ft)

Popular myths about the Great Pyramids

 Food kept inside the pyramids does not rot.

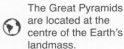 The Great Pyramids are located at the centre of the Earth's landmass.

 The Great Pyramid's height is related to the distance from the Earth to the Sun.

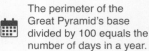 The perimeter of the Great Pyramid's base divided by 100 equals the number of days in a year.

GREAT SPHINX OF GIZA
A statue of a sphinx, a mythical animal usually depicted as a lion with the head of a man or bird.

Name
The Arabic term 'Sphinx' means 'Terrifying One' or 'Father of Dread'.

Face
It probably represents the Pharaoh Khafre.

Missing nose
The myth that the nose was destroyed by a Napoleonic cannonball is not true: it was already missing in sketches from 1757.

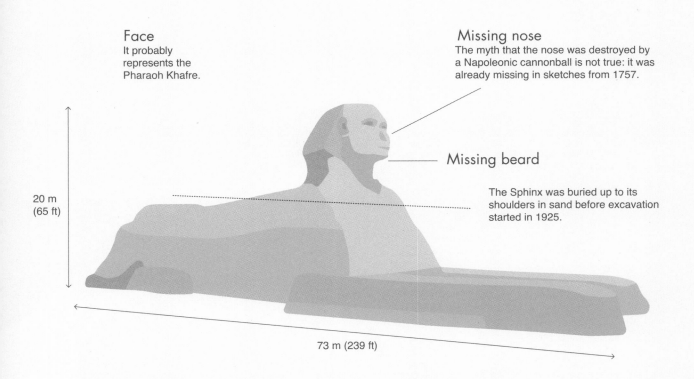

Missing beard

The Sphinx was buried up to its shoulders in sand before excavation started in 1925.

20 m (65 ft)

73 m (239 ft)

Mystery
No inscriptions describing the Sphinx's purpose or details of its construction have ever been found.

Pyramids' rock
The Sphinx was carved in a limestone rock from which blocks were probably forged to build the neighbouring pyramids.

Precise location
The monument was built so that it faces directly east.

Pigment
Traces of red, yellow and blue pigment have been found on the Sphinx leading some to think it was once coloured.

Restoration
Erosion of the monument has led to repairs being carried out by the Egyptian government.

87

SUEZ CANAL

Egypt

Construction: 10 years (1859–1869)

The Suez Canal is one of the world's most important waterways and it revolutionised sea transport, slicing thousands of miles off some of the most popular trade routes. It cuts through the Sinai Peninsula for 193.30 km (120.11 miles) to link the Mediterranean and Red seas. Around 8 per cent of all world sea trade is carried through the canal.

Specifications
Length: 193.30 km (originally 164 km)
Maximum draught of ships: 20.1 m (69.2 ft)
Maximum beam of ships: 50 m (164 ft)
Maximum depth: 24 m (78 ft)
Maximum deadweight tonnage: 200,000 tonnes

Mediterranean Sea
The world's fifth-largest sea.

Shortcut
It shortens the water voyage from, for example, London to the Arabian Sea by 8,900 kilometres (5,500 miles).

Port Said
The city was established in 1859 when construction of the canal started. Since then, canal trade has helped the city grow to reach its current population of over 600,000.

Mubarak Peace Bridge
This road bridge connecting Asia with Africa is the only permanent crossing over the canal. It has a 70-metre (23-feet) clearance for larger ships to sail beneath it.

Al-Kantara

Traffic
In 2017, 17,550 ships passed along the canal; 1,932 were not carrying any cargo.

Price war
The Suez and Panama canals fight for customers and offer discounts for large tanker ships.

Ismailia
Another city founded during the construction of the canal (1863).

Convention of Constantinople
This 1888 treat allows every ship to use the canal, whatever flag it flies, in both war and peace time.

Lake Timsah
Also known as Crocodile Lake. In prehistoric times, the Red Sea ended here.

No locks
As the sea level difference between its ends is minor, the canal required no locks. This made it easier to build than the Panama Canal.

Canal of the Pharaohs
This forerunner of the current canal once linked the Nile to the Red Sea. Construction probably started in the 6th century BCE.

Sinai Peninsula

This land bridge between Africa and Asia has always had strategic importance and has seen many armed conflicts over the years.

Revenue

In 2018, the canal earned a record high revenue of $5.585 billion.

Past projects

The idea of connecting the two seas has been of interest to many states throughout history including: Ancient Egypt, Persia, Venice, the Ottoman Empire, and France.

Napoleon's project

In 1798 Napoleon was interested in building a canal here, but he was wrongly told there was a 10 m (32 ft) difference in the two sea levels. The cost of mitigating this put him off the idea.

Bitter Lakes

These act as a passing place for ships using the Suez Canal.

Suez Crisis

The canal was owned by Britain and France until 1956, when Egypt nationalised it. Israel, the UK and France invaded the Sinai Peninsula to regain control of the canal, but international political pressure forced them to retreat.

Great Bitter Lake

Before the canal was built this was a dry salt valley.

Small Bitter Lake

Egyptian economy

Today, fees for ships' passage through the channel are a very important source of revenue for Egypt's budget and constitute around 2 per cent of its nominal GDP.

Suez

With large petrochemical plants and oil refineries, Suez is an unloading port for tankers carrying oil from the Persian Gulf. From here, oil is distributed by pipeline to other parts of Egypt.

Red Sea

The world's northernmost tropical sea has one of the highest water temperatures at 22°C (71°F).

OUARZAZATE SOLAR POWER STATION

Ouarzazate, Morocco
Construction: 6 years (2013–2019)

High in the Atlas Mountains of Morocco lies the Ouarzazate solar power station – the biggest solar thermal power plant in the world. It covers an area of 2,500 hectares (6,177 acres), which is equivalent to 3,500 football pitches. The design and construction teams overcame numerous technical challenges to create this model of sustainability in the high desert.

Construction
The plant was built in four phases: Noor 1, Noor 2, Noor 3 and Noor 4 (outside illustration).

The largest
Ouarzazate is the world's largest solar thermal power plant by electrical capacity.

Solar power tower
This central tower is 250 m (820 ft) high.

Mirrors
7,400 mirrors are arrayed in a concentric pattern to reflect light in the direction of the central tower.

Name
The complex is also known as the Noor Power Station – noor is Arabic for 'light'.

Capacity
The plant has an electrical capacity of 580 MW, which can meet about 5 per cent of Morocco's electricity demand.

Molten salt
The plant stores energy by heating molten salt. This stored heat means the plant can produce energy even at night.

Water consumption
Although the plant produces renewable energy, it uses between 2.5–3 million m³ (88–105 million ft²) of water per year for cleaning mirrors and solar panels.

Noor 3
Mirrors are arrayed around a solar power tower to focus sunlight on the collector on top of the tower. Liquid in the collector is heated, producing steam that drives a turbine to generate electricity. It has a capacity of 150 MW.

Cost
The total cost of the project is estimated at $9 billion.

Noor 2
Like Noor 1, it uses a parabolic trough as a solar thermal collector. It has a capacity of 200 MW.

Rows of parabolic trough collectors

Noor 1
Has a capacity of 160 MW.

BIBLIOTHECA ALEXANDRINA

Alexandria, Egypt

Construction: 7 years (1995–2002)

The Bibliotecha Alexandrina is a cultural achievement on a colossal scale.
The library complex includes six specialist libraries, a conference centre,
and room for 8 million books. The project was designed to commemorate
the fabled Library of Alexandria, which was lost in antiquity, and to create
a flourishing new centre for learning and research.

Alexandria

Egypt's second-largest city, with a population of
5.2 million people, was founded by Alexander
the Great in 331 BCE. It was here that the
Lighthouse of Alexandria, one of the Seven
Wonders of the Ancient World, was located.

Library of Alexandria

The largest library of the ancient world,
with as many as 700,000 objects, was
founded in the 3rd century BCE by the
ruler of Egypt, Ptolemy I Soter.

Walls

The façade of the library
is covered with more
than 6,000 granite panels
on which letters from 120
different alphabets have
been carved.

Symbolism

The shape of the building was
inspired by sunrise over the
Mediterranean Sea.

Destruction

The ancient library was
accidentally set on fire by
Julius Caesar in 48 BCE during
the Great Roman Civil War.

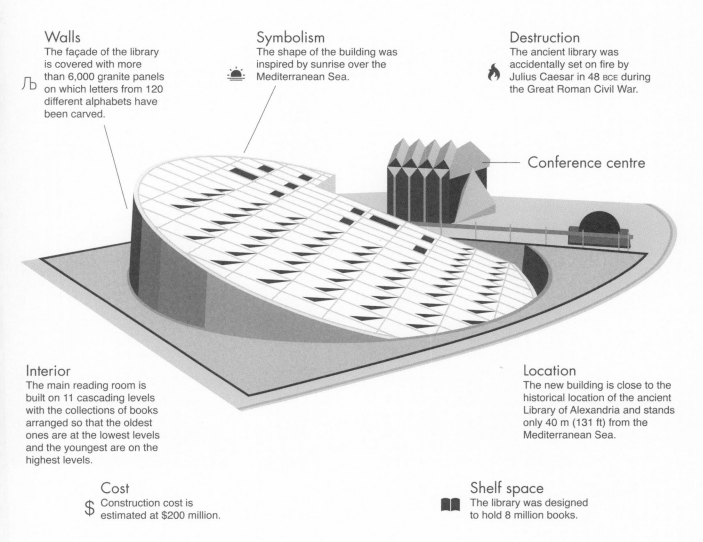

Conference centre

Interior

The main reading room is
built on 11 cascading levels
with the collections of books
arranged so that the oldest
ones are at the lowest levels
and the youngest are on the
highest levels.

Location

The new building is close to the
historical location of the ancient
Library of Alexandria and stands
only 40 m (131 ft) from the
Mediterranean Sea.

Cost

Construction cost is
estimated at $200 million.

Shelf space

The library was designed
to hold 8 million books.

Online backup

The Bibliotheca Alexandrina was the
site of the first external backup of the
Internet Archive.

Facilities

The library contains a planetarium, four
museums, four art galleries, map rooms
and a restoration laboratory, among others.

GREAT MOSQUE OF DJENNÉ

Djenné, Mali
Construction: c.13th century (reconstructed 1906–1907)

With its stylised mud walls, towers and pillars, the Great Mosque of Djenné is an instantly recognisable icon of African architecture. The mosque is located in the city of Djenné, Mali, which was a major trading centre between the 15th and 17th centuries. The rich caravans of the trans-Saharan routes carried salt, gold, and slaves through here and the town became a centre of Islamic scholarship.

Massive in mud
The mosque is the largest mud-brick building in the world.

Reconstruction
In 1906, the authorities decided to rebuild the ruined, 13th-century mosque that stood on this site. It is not exactly known how much the new design corresponds to the original and how much European architecture influenced the reconstruction.

Constant reconstruction
Every year the locals organise a repair festival, where teams of workers fill in cracks and patch up the outer plaster to ready the mosque for the annual monsoon.

Risky location
The mosque lies on the flood plain of the 1,100-km-long (683 miles) Bani River, the main tributary of the Niger River. This puts the structure at risk from the annual floods.

Disadvantaged
Mali is one of the world's poorest countries, with the fourth-highest fertility rate and seventh-highest infant mortality rate of any nation. 47 per cent of the population is under 14.

Central tower

Drainage
Ceramic half-pipes carry rainwater out beyond the edge of the roof to stop it running down the walls.

Materials
The walls are made of sun-baked bricks covered with plaster to create a smooth exterior.

Reinforcing platform
The mosque is built on a 3 m (10 ft) high platform to protect it when the river floods.

Original site
On the site of the mosque originally stood the palace of Sultan Kuburu, who, after converting to Islam, ordered it demolished and this temple built.

Bird inhabitants

Before the reconstruction in the early 20th century the ruins were home to thousands of swallows.

First description
The mosque was first described in a European publication in 1828, when its large size and declining condition were noted.

World Heritage Site
The mosque and the Old Towns of Djenné were added to the UNESCO World Heritage list in 1988.

Prayers
Today, the imam leads the prayers from inside the central tower. In the past, a crier standing on the top of the tower would call the prayer to people outside.

Architecture style
The mosque is considered the greatest example of Sudanese-style architecture that has developed since the 13th century.

Wooden reinforcement
Djenné citizens have opposed any modernisation of the building to maintain its historic integrity.

The walls are 1 m (3 ft) thick

Market
A weekly market takes place in the square in front of the mosque.

Recognition
The mosque features on the coat of arms of Mali.

Facing east
The prayer wall of the mosque faces east towards Mecca.

The towers of the Taj Mahal
lean slightly outwards so that
if an earthquake hit, they
would not fall on the tomb.

Asia

ANGKOR WAT

Siem Reap, Cambodia
Construction: 12th century

The largest religious monument in the world, Angkor Wat is also one of the most beautiful and technically impressive. The temple complex once stood at the heart of a thriving city that ruled over a vast and wealthy empire. One of history's architectural marvels, it would have taken thousands of workers 30 years to quarry, transport, carve and erect the millions of sandstone blocks that form the complex.

Angkor Wat was named a UNESCO World Heritage Site in 1992, and was proclaimed one of the New Seven Wonders of the World in 2007.

Angkor
The temple lies in the ruins of Angkor, former capital city of the Khmer Empire, which ruled from 1010 to 1220. At its peak, Angkor was larger than modern-day Paris.

Etymology
The name Angkor Wat means 'City of Temples' in Cambodian.

Khmer Empire
This powerful Hindu-Buddhist empire ruled most of mainland Southeast Asia.

The largest
This Cambodian temple is the largest religious structure in the world, occupying 162.6 hectares (401 acres).

Hydraulic city
The city of Angkor had a network of moats, canals and irrigation ponds that was very advanced for its time.

Symbolism
The walls and moat surrounding the temple symbolise the ocean and mountains surrounding Mount Meru.

Floating stones
The stones for Angkor Wat were quarried 40 km (25 miles) away and brought here by canal.

Moat
200 m (656 ft) wide

Facing west
Unlike other Khmer temples, Angkor Wat is oriented to the west. This may reflect its dedication to Vishnu, the deity associated with the west.

Divine temple
In contrast to previous Khmer temples, Angkor Wat was dedicated to the Hindu god Vishnu rather than to a king.

Angkor Sankranta
A large festival celebrating Khmer New Year takes place in the ruins of Angkor every April.

Tourism
Angkor Wat is a destination for over 50 per cent of tourists visiting Cambodia

National symbol
Angkor Wat features on the Cambodian flag.

Central tower
65 m tall, this was considered the house of the gods. Today it is a Buddhist sanctuary.

Mount Meru
The temple represents this sacred Hindu mountain with the central quincunx of five towers symbolising the five peaks of the mountain.

Angkor Wat style
The temple gave its name to the classical style of Khmer architecture.

Sandstone
The temple was built from 5–10 million sandstone blocks, weighing up to 1.5 tonnes each.

Steep stairs
Some stairways inside the temple are inclined at a head-spinning 70 degrees, and represent 'stairways to heaven'.

Towers
Their shape resembles a lotus flower.

Bas-reliefs
Almost every wall in the temple features complex carvings. The bas-reliefs depict scenes from mythology and royal life.

Third level
Accessed only by the king and highest priests.

Second level
Its walls are decorated with over 1,500 reliefs depicting celestial dancers.

First level
This area was open to commoners.

Harmony
The building's architecture is characterised by its perfect balance of elements, their arrangement and proportions.

Sinking
The temple is at risk of sinking as a result of increased groundwater extraction to meet the needs of the growing local population and international visitors.

Shift in religion

Originally a hindu temple, it was transformed into a Buddhist place of worship several dozen years after its construction.

GREAT WALL OF CHINA

China, Mongolia, Russia, North Korea

Construction: 7th century BCE–16th century CE

The longest structure on Earth, the Great Wall is one of the most impressive architectural feats in history. This series of fortifications stretches for thousands of miles along the ancient northern borders of China and was built to keep out invasions by nomadic tribes.

The Great Wall was listed as a UNESCO World Heritage Site in 1987 and was declared one of the New Seven Wonders of the World in 2007.

End of construction

After the Qing Dynasty conquered China, the Empire's borders expanded north. The Great Wall was inside the country and its further development became unnecessary.

Ming Great Wall

The larger part of the wall existing today was constructed during the Ming Dynasty (1368–1644). These fortifications are 8,850 km (5,500 miles) long.

Lost miles

Around 22 per cent of the wall built during the Ming Dynasty has been lost.

> ↝ – Ming Dynasty Great Wall
> ⋰ – other parts of the Great Wall

Great Wall of Qi

The oldest existing part of the Great Wall. Its construction began in 685 BCE.

MONGOLIA

Destruction and demolition

In the popular tourist spots the wall has been renovated, but in many remote areas its stones have been stolen for building. It has also suffered from graffiti and vandalism.

JIAYU PASS

Beijing

NORTH KOREA

SHANHAI PASS

BADALING GREAT WALL

CHINA

Visible from low Earth orbit

NASA notes that the wall is visible from space (at an altitude of 160 km (99 miles)), although astronauts say that conditions have to be absolutely perfect.

Length

A 2012 archeological survey found that, in total, all the wall's sections are 21,196 km (13,170 miles) long, more than half of the length of the equator.

Defensive function

The wall was built to protect the northern parts of the Chinese empires against the invasions of the Great Steppe nomadic groups.

Visible from the Moon

One of the world's most widespread myths, dating back to 1754, says that the wall is visible from the moon with the naked eye. However, the structure is so narrow that this would be the same as seeing a human hair from a distance of 3 km (1.8 miles).

Great Wall of China hoax

This fake story from 1899 claimed American companies had contracts to tear down the wall and build a road instead. An urban legend grew that the 1900 Boxer Rebellion arose from these articles.

Great Wall Marathon

One of the world's most challenging marathons. Its arduous course has more than 20,000 stone steps and a continually changing gradient.

First European description

Europeans heard about the Wall for the first time in 1563 after João de Barros, a Portuguese historian, described it in his work *Décadas da Ásia*.

JIAYU PASS
The westernmost border fortress of the Ming Dynasty section of the Great Wall.

Invasion threat
The pass was built around 1372 to hold back an invasion by Timur, a conqueror from Central Asia. However Timur died while leading his army towards China.

Bricks
Legend says that exactly 99,999 bricks were used in the construction of the pass. One additional brick is symbolically placed loose on one of the gates.

Made of earth
Like much of the wall, Jiayu Pass was partially made of rammed earth.

11 m
(36 ft)

SHANHAI PASS
This fortress lies at the far eastern end of the wall where it meets the sea.

Key to the Capitals
It is close to Shenyang and Beijing, the capital cities of Manchuria and China.

Battle of Shanhai Pass
In 1644, after the fall of the Ming Dynasty, forces of the Qing Dynasty defeated a rebel army at the Shanhai Pass. This marked the beginning of the last imperial dynasty of China.

14 m
(46 ft)

BADALING GREAT WALL
In 1957, this was the first part of the Wall opened to the public by the People's Republic of China. Today, it is probably the most famous section.

Watchtowers
Around 25,000 watchtowers were built on the Ming section of wall. They were sited on hills to increase their visibility and for their ability to transmit signals in the event of an attack.

This part of the wall reaches an altitude of 1015 m (3,330 ft) above sea level and offers panoramic views of the hills.

Battlements
Most of the wall had these as protection for guards; they were usually 2 m (6.3 ft) tall and 1.5 m (4.9 ft) wide.

FORBIDDEN CITY

Beijing, China

Construction: 14 years (1406–1420)

The Forbidden City is a palace complex that, for almost 500 years, was both the home of the Chinese emperor and the ceremonial and political centre of government.

The architecture and art of the complex has had a deep cultural influence throughout Asia. The Forbidden City was recognised for its unique cultural and historical treasures by UNESCO when the organisation declared it a World Heritage Site in 1987. It is also listed as having the largest collection of preserved ancient wooden structures in the world.

Emperor's residence
The complex served as an imperial palace for the rulers of the Ming and Qing dynasties (1368–1912). It was home to 24 emperors.

Etymology
The name 'Forbidden City' came from the custom that no one could enter or leave the palace without the emperor's permission.

紫禁城
The name 'Forbidden City' written in Chinese characters.

Area
The city covers an area of 72 hectares (178 acres) and has 980 buildings with over 8,866 rooms.

Wall
7.9 m (26 ft) tall
8.62 m (28 ft) wide

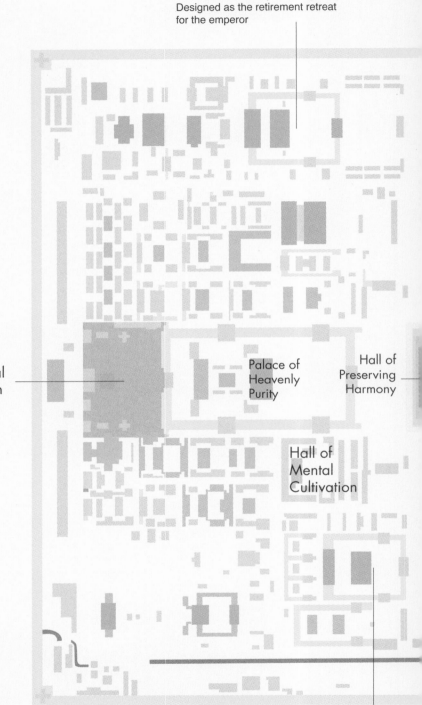

Palace of Tranquil Longevity
Designed as the retirement retreat for the emperor

Imperial Garden

Palace of Heavenly Purity

Hall of Preserving Harmony

Hall of Mental Cultivation

Palace of Compassion and Tranquility
This was originally the residence of the empress.

Visitors
16.7 million tourists
visited the site in 2017.

Wooden structures
The complex houses the
world's largest collection
of preserved ancient
wooden structures.

Artefacts
1.8 million cultural relics
are stored in the Forbidden
City, around 50,000 of
which are paintings.

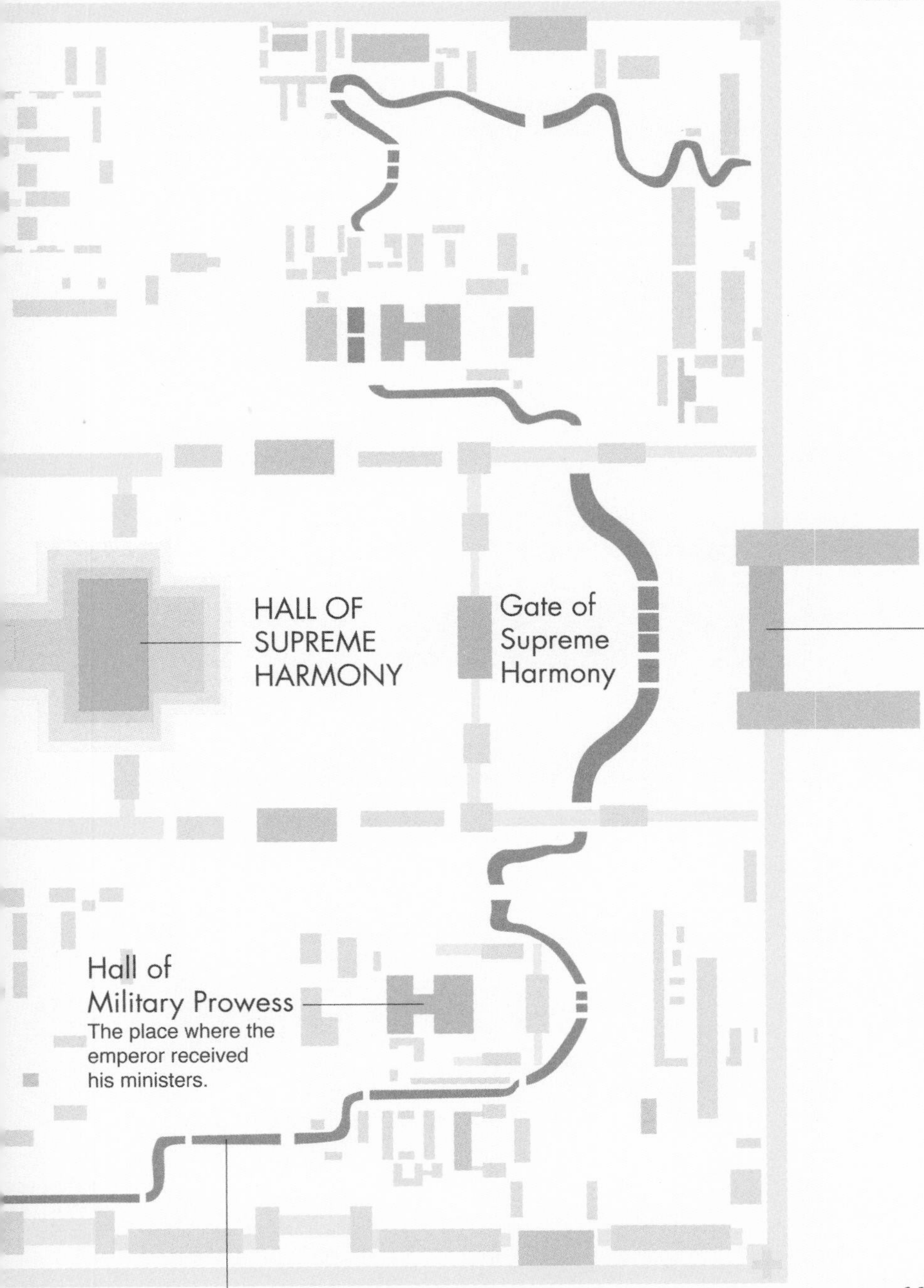

**HALL OF
SUPREME
HARMONY**

**Gate of
Supreme
Harmony**

MERIDIAN GATE

Yellow tiles
As yellow is the colour of the
emperor, all but two buildings
in the Forbidden City have
roofs covered with yellow tiles.

**Hall of
Military Prowess**
The place where the
emperor received
his ministers.

Roof-figures
The number of statues placed on roofs
is a guide to the importance of the
building. The Hall of Supreme Harmony
is the only building with 10 roof-figures.

**Golden
Water River**
An artificial stream that
runs through the city.

HALL OF SUPREME HARMONY

This is the largest hall of the Forbidden City and the largest surviving wooden structure in China.

Original construction

The Hall of Supreme Harmony was built in 1406 by the Ming dynasty.

Name change

In the past, the hall has been named *Fengtian Dian* and *Huangji Dian*. It's current name was given by the Shunzhi Emperor of the Qing dynasty in 1645.

Ceremonial function

The hall was used for the coronations and weddings of emperors, and during the Ming Dynasty the emperor held courts here.

Fire

The hall has been destroyed by fire and rebuilt seven times.

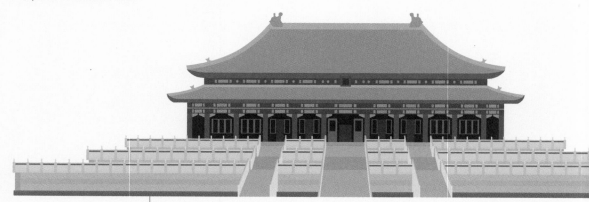

Marble base

The hall is set atop three levels of ornamental marble.

Ramps

One of the ramps that leads to the upper terrace is carved from a single block of stone 16.57 metres (54.4 ft) long, 3.07 metres (10.1 ft) wide, and 1.7 metres (5.6 ft) thick. It weighs 200 tonnes and is the largest carved block in China.

9:5

The ratio of the width to the depth of the building is 9 to 5 and these numbers are attributed to the emperor.

Qing dynasty throne

Inside the Hall of Supreme Harmony, there is a throne made of red sandalwood. Emperors of the Qing dynasty used this throne.

Dragon

Above the throne is an intricate panel depicting a dragon. In its mouth is a set of metal balls called the Xuanyuan Mirror. If someone were to usurp the throne, it is believed that the dragon would drop the balls in order to kill them.

MERIDIAN GATE

The largest gate of the Forbidden City complex. Today it serves as the only entrance to the complex for tourists.

Imposing structure

The Meridian Gate is almost 40 metres tall, making it an imposing structure. Its central tower, at 60 metres, has a double roof covered in coloured glazed tiles.

Towers

Arrangements of gate's five towers depicts the image of a flying phoenix.

Announcements

The emperor's laws and proclamations were announced from this gate.

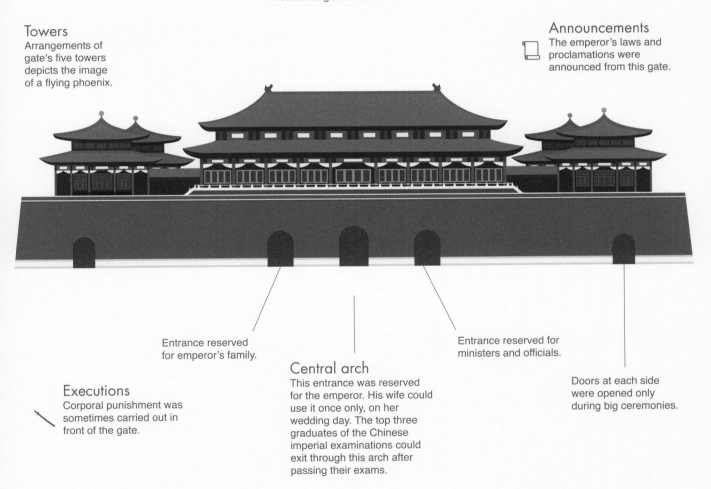

Entrance reserved for emperor's family.

Entrance reserved for ministers and officials.

Executions

Corporal punishment was sometimes carried out in front of the gate.

Central arch

This entrance was reserved for the emperor. His wife could use it once only, on her wedding day. The top three graduates of the Chinese imperial examinations could exit through this arch after passing their exams.

Doors at each side

were opened only during big ceremonies.

Arms

The Meridian Gate has two arms – one on either side. The arms are made from 'que towers' which are decorative ceremonial gate towers.

The Meridian

Chinese emperors believed that they should live at the centre of the universe as they were *Sons of Heaven*. They thought that the Meridian went through the middle of the gate, so they decided to build the Forbidden City symmetrically to this Meridian line.

THREE GORGES DAM

China

Construction: 9 years (1994–2003)

This colossal hydroelectric gravity dam is the world's largest power station by output capacity. With its reservoir it forms a structure so large that it alters the rotation of the planet.

Planned for decades, it is a highly symbolic achievement for China. Its turbine technology is among the most advanced in the world; it has decreased greenhouse gas emissions and delivered widespread economic benefits.

Largest power station

With a capacity of 22,500 MW, it is the world's largest power station. It can produce almost three times more energy than the world's largest nuclear plant, Kashiwazaki-Kariwa in Japan.

Flood control

One of the dam's main functions is to control seasonal downstream flooding, reducing its frequency from once every 10 years to once every 100 years.

Green energy

The project was part of China's strategy to limit greenhouse gas emissions.

Yangtze

At 6,380 km (3,964 miles) long, the Yangtze is the world's third-longest river and is the sixth-largest by discharge volume.

Spillway capacity

Every second water that would fill 46 Olympic-size pools (116,000 m³) pours out.

Generators

The plant has 34 generators. The largest weighs around 6,000 tonnes, which is equivalent to 32 blue whales.

Turbines

Its 10 m (33 ft) wide turbines rotate at 75 revolutions per minute.

Construction cost

Costing $31.765 billion, it is one of the most expensive projects in human history.

Construction material

The dam is mostly made of concrete and steel. The steel used could build 63 Eiffel Towers.

Mao Ze-dong's project

The project was strongly supported by the Chinese dictator and he even wrote a poem about it. Some engineers were imprisoned for criticising the project.

Coal alternative

At its full power, the dam produces the equivalent of energy obtained from 31 million tonnes of coal annually.

Untapped potential

Although it has the greatest potential electricity production of all dams, it runs at only around 45 per cent of its capacity. The world record in actual energy production belongs to South America's Itaipu Dam.

Increasing electricity consumption

Three Gorges Dam was planned to meet 10 per cent of China's electricity demand, but with rising consumption, in 2015 it provided only 2.5 per cent.

Water level management

The dam and its reservoir can control the water level downstream. During the rainy season it retains water which it releases during the dry season for agriculture and irrigation purposes.

Area

The reservoir has a surface area of 1,084 km² (673.5 miles), which is twice the size of Lake Geneva.

Water level

The maximum water level in the reservoir is 175 m (574 ft) above sea level.

Ship lift

The dam's ship lift allows large ships to travel further upriver. The dam increased the Yangtze's barge capacity sixfold, and cut carbon dioxide emissions by 630,000 tonnes.

Three Gorges Reservoir

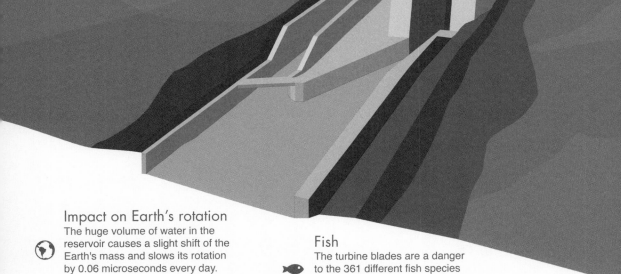

Impact on Earth's rotation

The huge volume of water in the reservoir causes a slight shift of the Earth's mass and slows its rotation by 0.06 microseconds every day.

Fish

The turbine blades are a danger to the 361 different fish species living in the river.

Relocation

The construction of the dam resulted in the relocation of approximately 1.3 million people living in 13 cities, 140 towns, and over 1,600 villages that had to be flooded.

Chinese river dolphin

The dam contributed to the extinction of this species of freshwater dolphin.

Earthquake risk

Despite its resistance to earthquakes, the dam sits on a seismic fault and its collapse would threaten the lives of hundreds of millions of people.

TAIPEI 101

Taipei, Taiwan

Construction: 5 years (1999–2004)

Taipei 101 is an iconic building of Taiwan and for six years was the tallest building in the world, stretching 52 m nearer to the heavens than the Petronas Towers.

The tower's advanced design makes it the largest 'green' building in the world and it is also the safest structure in a region known for earthquakes.

Water recycling
A recycling system on the roof and façade of the building collect enough water to meet 30 per cent of the building's needs.

Tuned mass damper
This enormous steel sphere hanging from wires at the top of the skyscraper acts as a giant pendulum, countering the movement of the building during earthquakes. At 6 m in diameter and weighing 660 tonnes, Taipei 101's mass damper is the largest and heaviest in the world.

Earthquakes
Taiwan lies in the Pacific Rim, which is a major earthquake zone. Various features ensure that when the Earth shakes, Taipei 101 is the safest place in the whole country.

World's tallest building
The skyscraper was the world's tallest building from 2004 to 2010, when the Burj Khalifa was completed.

101
The building has exactly 101 floors, hence its name.

Skyscraper
Every building must meet two conditions to be called a skyscraper. It has to be taller than 150 m and have over 40 floors.

Accident

During construction in 2002, a 6.8-magnitude earthquake hit Taipei. The building was not damaged, but two cranes mounted at the 56th floor toppled, killing five people.

Typhoon

As there are many tropical cyclones in this region, Taipei 101 was designed to withstand winds of 216 km/h (134 mph).

"Green" building

Since 2011, Taipei 101 has been the tallest and largest 'green' building with Leadership in Energy and Environmental Design (LEED) Platinum certification in the world.

Glass

An advanced glass curtain wall blocks heat and UV and reduces the impact of the outside temperature by 50 per cent.

508 m
(1,666 ft)

Number 8

The building has eight main sections; eight is the luckiest number in Chinese culture and symbolises prosperity and success.

Elevators

Its elevators travel at 60.6 km/h (37.7 mph)

Fireworks

101 is famous for its New Year's Eve fireworks show, which lights up the entire building.

TAJ MAHAL

Agra, India
Construction: 17 years (1631–1648)

A masterpiece of design and an icon of India, beauty and love, the Taj Mahal is one of the world's most famous buildings. It is considered the jewel of Muslim art in India and was nominated as one of the New Seven Wonders of the World in 2007.

The Taj Mahal attracts more than 7 million visitors a year. It was designated as a UNESCO World Heritage Site in 1983.

Black Taj Mahal
Legend says that the emperor Shah Jahan wanted to build a mausoleum across the river that would be a reflection of the original but in black marble.

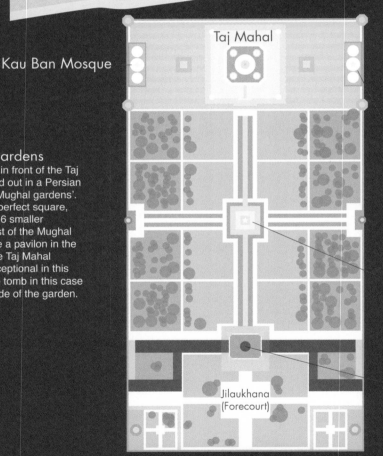

Yamuna river
1,370 km (855 miles) long, it rises in glaciers at a height of 6,387 m (20,955 ft). It is the second-largest tributary of the Ganges.

Kau Ban Mosque

Taj Mahal

Threat
Pollution in the river has been turning the Taj Mahal yellow. The river also threatens the mausoleum with a wash.

"Jawab" (answer)
Some sources say that this building was built only to be a reflection of the Kau Ban mosque to create balance.

Mughal gardens
The gardens in front of the Taj Mahal are laid out in a Persian style called 'Mughal gardens'. They form a perfect square, divided into 16 smaller squares. Most of the Mughal gardens have a pavilon in the centre but the Taj Mahal garden is exceptional in this regard as the tomb in this case is from the side of the garden.

River representation
According to Islam, in paradise there are four rivers flowing from a central point on the mountain. They represent water, milk, wine and honey.

Great Gate
Symbolic gateway to the paradise.

Jilaukhana
(Forecourt)

Pollution
Agra is one of the world's most polluted cities.

Directly behind the walls of the Taj Mahal is an extremely densely populated district of the city.

Beloved wife
It was built as a tomb to honour Mughal emperor Shah Jahan's second and favourite wife, Mumtaz Mahal. She died while giving birth to their fourteenth child.

New Wonder of the World
In 2007, the Taj Mahal was declared one of the New Seven Wonders of the World.

Taj Mahal Diamond
This famous jewel used to belong to Mumtaz Mahal. Centuries later, the actor Richard Burton gifted it to the actress Elizabeth Taylor.

Dome
The tomb's most spectacular feature is 35 m (115 ft) tall.

Towers
The 40 m (131 ft) tall towers lean slightly outwards so that if an earthquake hit, they would not fall on the tomb.

Balcony
The muezzin calls the faithful to prayer from here.

Plant ornaments
The Taj Mahal's decorations are especially famous for the sculptures of 46 different species of plant.

Gems
28 types of gems were used for the decoration of the Taj Mahal.

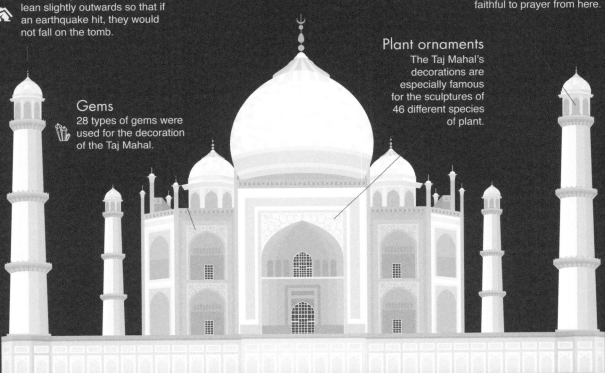

Black marble?
Air, polluted with dust and carbon, is darkening the white marble walls of the Taj Mahal.

Dust storms
100 km/h (62 mph) dust storms add to the damage to the walls of the mausoleum.

Elephants
More than 1,000 elephants were used in the construction of the building.

Made of marble?
The building is actually made of red sandstone bricks covered with marble as protection from corrosion.

Colours
The marble used for construction has a magical ability to reflect the colour of the sky, changing from red and orange to blue and purple.

Materials
Materials used for construction were brought from areas that today lie in India, Pakistan, Afghanistan, Tibet, Sri Lanka, China and the Arabian Peninsula.

OLD CITY (JERUSALEM)

Jerusalem, Israel
Construction: 11th century BCE

For three of the world's major religions – Christianity, Islam and Judaism – this ancient city is one of the holiest places on Earth. The proximity of these faiths and their followers has led to tension and indeed violence over the centuries. Nevertheless, the Old City is a living historic treasure, a place where spirituality and the sublime are written on the stones themselves. Jerusalem is a city like no other; its ancient heart was added to the UNESCO World Heritage List in 1981.

Golgotha
Another possible location of the hill where Jesus was crucified.

Church of the Holy Sepulchre
It contains the two holiest sites in Christianity: the area known as Calvary or Golgotha, where Jesus was crucified; and Jesus's empty tomb, where he is said to have been buried and resurrected.

Damascus Gate
Leads to an ancient road to Damascus.

New Gate
Old City's youngest gate, built in 1889.

Quarters
The Old City is traditionally divided into four ethnic quarters: Armenian, Christian, Jewish and Muslim.

Size
Until 1860, the relatively small Old City (it covers an area of just 0.9 km²) was the whole of the city of Jerusalem.

Jaffa Gate

Tower of David
This impressive citadel was destroyed many times before being rebuilt and expanded in the 16th century.

Monastery of Saint Mark
Possible location of the Last Supper of Christ and his disciples.

Sieges
The Old City has been besieged at least 15 times.

David's Tomb
Some consider this to be the burial site of David, second King of Israel, famous for killing Goliath.

Zion Gate

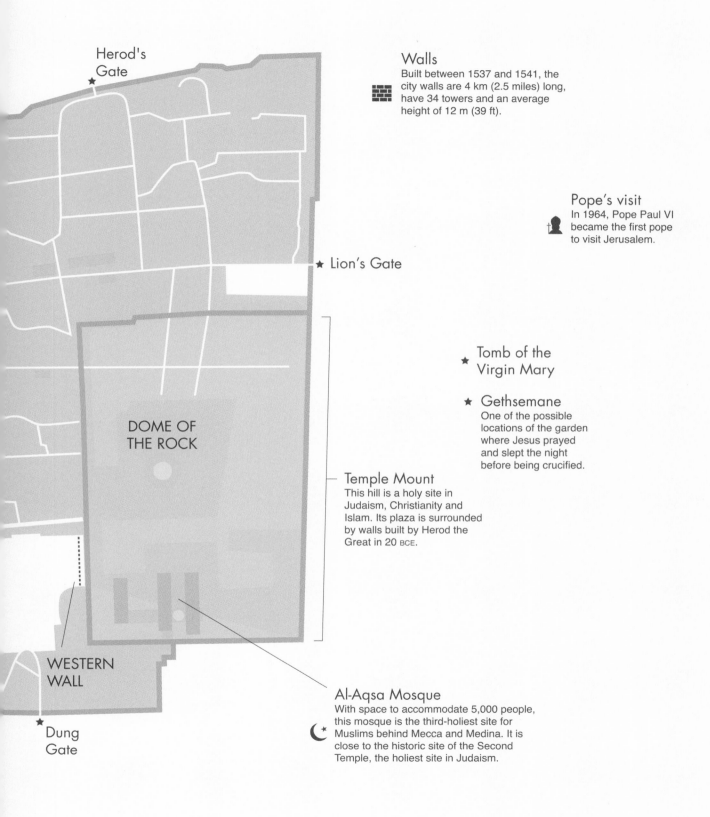

Herod's
Gate

Walls
Built between 1537 and 1541, the
city walls are 4 km (2.5 miles) long,
have 34 towers and an average
height of 12 m (39 ft).

Pope's visit
In 1964, Pope Paul VI
became the first pope
to visit Jerusalem.

★ Lion's Gate

**Tomb of the
Virgin Mary**

★ **Gethsemane**
One of the possible
locations of the garden
where Jesus prayed
and slept the night
before being crucified.

DOME OF
THE ROCK

Temple Mount
This hill is a holy site in
Judaism, Christianity and
Islam. Its plaza is surrounded
by walls built by Herod the
Great in 20 BCE.

WESTERN
WALL

Al-Aqsa Mosque
With space to accommodate 5,000 people,
this mosque is the third-holiest site for
Muslims behind Mecca and Medina. It is
close to the historic site of the Second
Temple, the holiest site in Judaism.

★ Dung
Gate

WESTERN WALL

Small fragment of the ancient wall that might have surrounded the Temple in Jerusalem.

Holy place

As this part of the wall is believed to be the part of the ancient Temple in Jerusalem, it is one of the most sacred places in Judaism.

Paper prayers

The wall is visited by millions of pilgrims from all over the world who stick pieces of paper containing prayers in the cracks between stones.

Material

Built from limestone rocks of various sizes, laid in different years.

Dome of the Rock

The wall surrounds one of Jerusalem's most recognisable landmarks, the Dome of the Rock.

Layers

There are 45 layers of stone laying on top of each other to create the western wall.

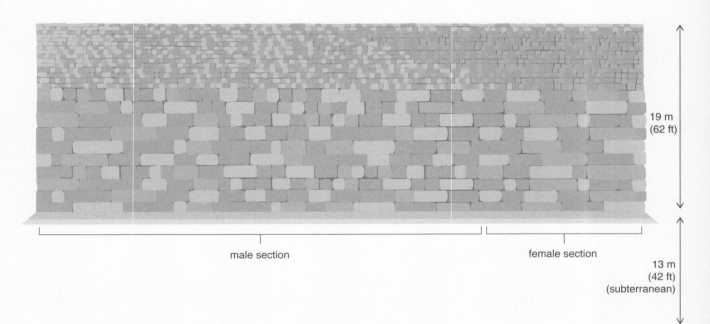

male section

female section

19 m
(62 ft)

13 m
(42 ft)
(subterranean)

Western Wall Plaza

The plaza in front of the wall can accommodate up to 60,000 people. It's a place of unrest on a religious background.

Division

Traditionally, in Judaism, women and men pray separately. The wall is therefore divided into two separate sections.

DOME OF THE ROCK
This Islamic Shrine was built between 688–692 CE. It is one of the holiest sites in Islam.

Foundation Stone
Inside the dome lies the holiest site in Judaism: a rock from which the world was created and where Adam was given life. Jews all over the world pray towards this spot. In Islam it is the place where Muhammad ascended into heaven in 621 CE.

Entry
Non-Muslims are not permitted to enter the Dome of the Rock.

Knights Templar
This Catholic military order, also known as 'Templum Domini', used the Dome of the Rock as its headquarters for much of the 12th century. The building was featured on the seals of Templar Grand Masters.

 The dome is probably the oldest example of Islamic architecture still surviving.

Its iconic gold-plated roof was added in 1959–1961.

Church
It was turned into a church after the Crusaders captured Jerusalem in 1099.

Sacrifice
It is believed that the Dome is built on the place that Abraham offered Isaac as a sacrifice.

Earthquake
The dome collapsed during an earthquake in 1015 and was rebuilt eight years later.

Mosaics
Its mosaic ornaments were added centuries after its construction and were inspired by nearby Byzantine churches.

No animals
The mosaics found within and surrounding the Dome exclude animal and human representations, due to Muslim laws forbidding the depiction of living beings.

PETRA

Ma'an Governorate, Jordan
Construction: c.5th century BCE

The majestic rock-carved, rose-red city of Petra, which amazes the 800,000 tourists that visit every year, is a legacy of the Nabataeans who settled in southern Jordan more than 2,000 years ago. The area became a major regional trading hub and the Nabataean Kingdom grew in power and wealth. It declined after new sea trade routes were established, and after an earthquake destroyed parts of it in 363 CE.

Today, Petra is one of the world's most famous landmarks. It was included in the UNESCO World Heritage Site list and it was named one of The New Seven Wonders of the World in 2007.

Rediscovery
Only a small number of nomads lived in Petra until it was rediscovered by Swiss traveller Johann Ludwig Burckhardt in 1812.

Gorge
To reach Petra, you walk along a narrow, dim, 1.2 km (0.7 mile) long gorge before suddenly emerging to see the splendour of the site.

AD DEIR
Also known as 'The Monastery', throughout history it fulfilled various social and religious functions.

Memorial
Ad Deir is thought to have been built as a memorial to Nabatean King Obodas I.

Architecture
It was constructed at the time of the Hellenistic and Roman Empires, as can be seen from its classical Greek-influenced architectural style.

45 m
(147 ft)

Columns
The columns are Corinthian in style and are decorative rather than structural.

The main chamber's door is 8 m (26 ft) high and provides the only entry for daylight into the interior.

Damage
This building has suffered more damage from erosion than its neighbour.

Church
From close up you can see crosses in the façade of the building that were carved when it was used as a church in Byzantine times.

Visitors
It's the second most visited landmark of Petra after Al-Khazneh.

AL-KHAZNEH
The most elaborate and famous temple of Petra, this was built as a crypt for Nabatean King Aretas IV Philopatris at the beginning of the 1st century CE.

The Treasury
19th-century Bedouins believed it contained hidden riches and called the building 'The Treasury'.

Urn
This is marked with bullet holes from locals who shot at it in the early 20th century believing that treasure was hidden within. They were out of luck – the urn is solid sandstone.

Eagles
Carvings of four eagles, which were said to carry souls away.

Amazons statues
On both sides of the upper level there are damaged statues of Amazons 'dancing' with double-axes.

Isis-Tyche
A carving of the goddess Isis-Tyche, goddess of fortune and prosperity.

Mythology
Generally, the sculptures of Al-Khazneh are of mythological heroes associated with the afterlife.

39 m
(128 ft)

Twins statues
Statues of Castor and Pollux, the twins who both lived partly on Olympus and partly in the underworld, stand at the entrance.

Sandstone
The building is carved out of a sandstone cliff. This is a relatively soft sedimentary rock.

Erosion
Many of the architectural details have been destroyed by erosion due to the relative softness of the sandstone.

PETRONAS TOWERS

Kuala Lumpur, Malaysia
Construction: 6 years (1993–1998)

For six years the Petronas Towers stood taller than every other building on the planet, until Taipei 101 took the title. The buildings are a famous landmark of Kuala Lumpur and are still the world's tallest twin towers.

World's tallest building
The towers were the tallest buildings in the world from 1998 to 2004 then surpassed by Taipei 101.

Petronas
The building houses the headquarters of Malaysian petroleum company Petronas, the 191st-largest company in the world.

Record jump
In 1999, Felix Baumgartner set a world record in BASE jumping when he leapt from the top of the building.

"Spiderman"
In 2009, Alain 'Spiderman' Robert climbed Tower Two in less than two hours. It was his third try – he was arrested before reaching the top on his first two attempts.

Up above
From a bird's eye view, the structure of the towers resembles the letter 'M' for Malaysia

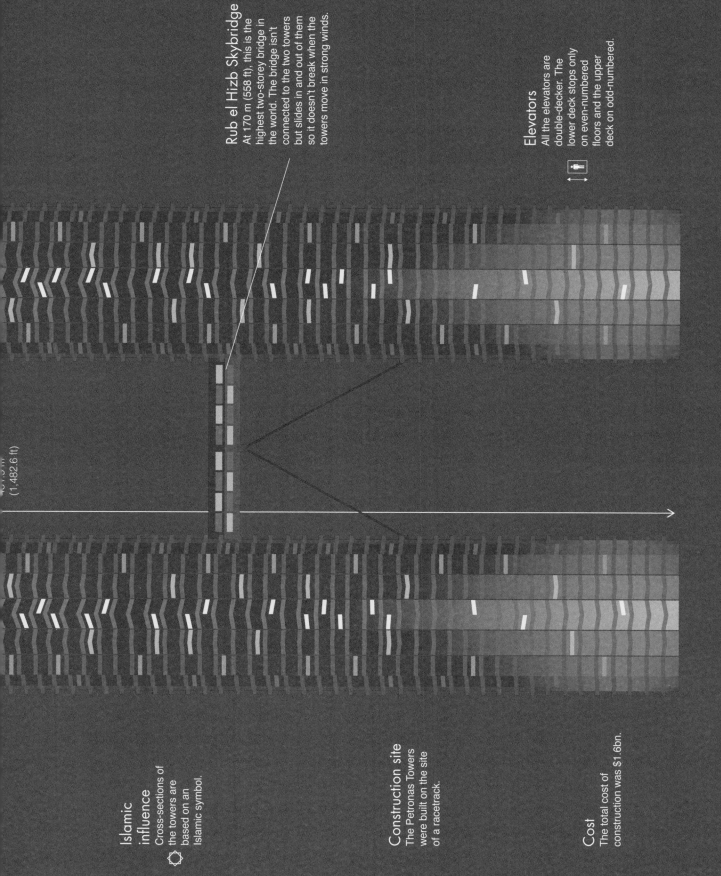

Rub el Hizb Skybridge
At 170 m (558 ft), this is the highest two-storey bridge in the world. The bridge isn't connected to the two towers but slides in and out of them so it doesn't break when the towers move in strong winds.

Elevators
All the elevators are double-decker. The lower deck stops only on even-numbered floors and the upper deck on odd-numbered.

Islamic influence
Cross-sections of the towers are based on an Islamic symbol.

Construction site
The Petronas Towers were built on the site of a racetrack.

Cost
The total cost of construction was $1.6bn.

451.9 m
(1,482.6 ft)

GREAT MOSQUE OF MECCA

Mecca, Saudi Arabia
Construction: Founded c.634, largely rebuilt in 1571

Mecca is the birthplace of Muḥammad and the site of his first revelation of the Quran. It is the holiest city in Islam. The Great Mosque is the largest mosque in the world and can accommodate 1.5 million worshippers. It is the destination for Muslims performing one of two pilgrimages: Hajj, which is mandatory for every believer at least once in their lives, and Umrah, a lesser pilgrimage that can be made at any time of the year.

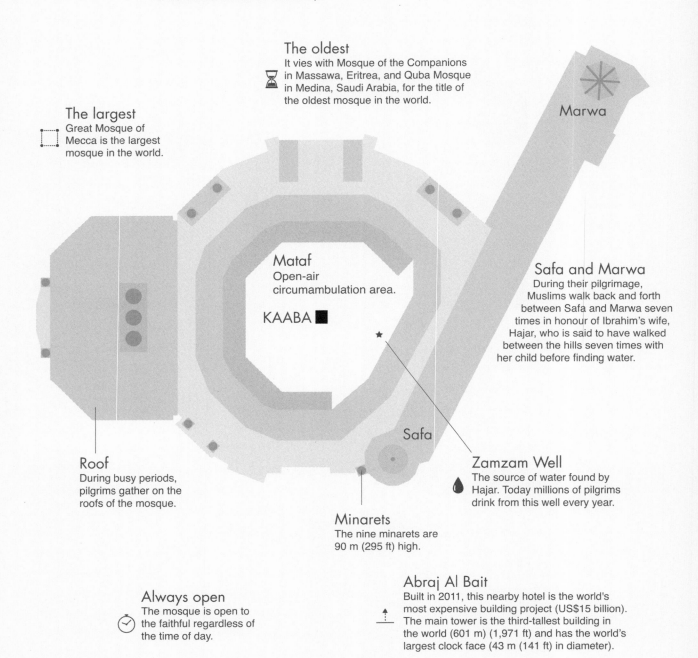

Ibrahim
Islamic prophet who is said to have lived for 169 years. According to Islam, he and his son Ishmael built the Kaaba as the world's first house of worship.

The oldest
It vies with Mosque of the Companions in Massawa, Eritrea, and Quba Mosque in Medina, Saudi Arabia, for the title of the oldest mosque in the world.

The largest
Great Mosque of Mecca is the largest mosque in the world.

Marwa

Mataf
Open-air circumambulation area.

KAABA ■

Safa and Marwa
During their pilgrimage, Muslims walk back and forth between Safa and Marwa seven times in honour of Ibrahim's wife, Hajar, who is said to have walked between the hills seven times with her child before finding water.

Safa

Roof
During busy periods, pilgrims gather on the roofs of the mosque.

Zamzam Well
The source of water found by Hajar. Today millions of pilgrims drink from this well every year.

Minarets
The nine minarets are 90 m (295 ft) high.

Always open
The mosque is open to the faithful regardless of the time of day.

Abraj Al Bait
Built in 2011, this nearby hotel is the world's most expensive building project (US$15 billion). The main tower is the third-tallest building in the world (601 m) (1,971 ft) and has the world's largest clock face (43 m (141 ft) in diameter).

KAABA
Its name translates as 'the Cube'. This granite building stands in the centre of the Great Mosque of Mecca. It is the holiest site in Islam and is considered to be the 'House of God'.

Corners
The four corners of the Kaaba are aligned towards the four cardinal points of the compass.

Qiblah
The Kaaba is the point towards which all the Muslims in the world face while praying.

Black Stone corner

Levantine corner

Yemeni corner

Iraqi corner

Band with Quranic text, including the Shahada, which is the Islamic declaration of faith, one of the Five Pillars of Islam.

Kiswah
Black curtain made of silk and gold that covers the Kaaba. It is replaced every year during the Hajj.

Entrance
These 300 kg (661 lb) doors are made of gold and are set 2.13 m (6.98 ft) above the ground.

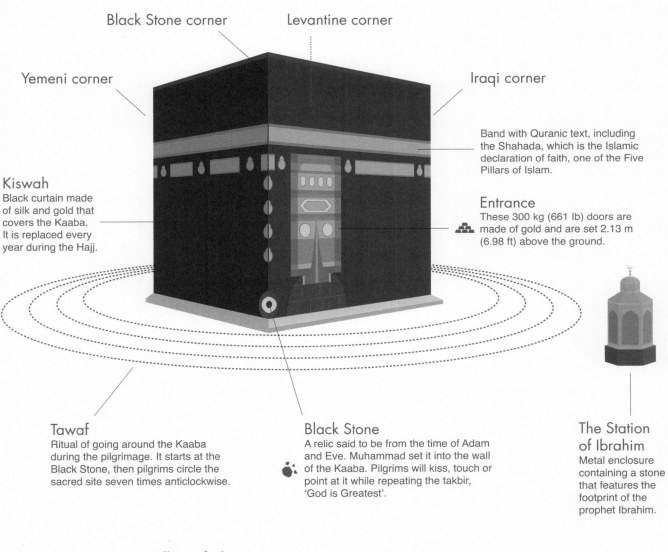

Tawaf
Ritual of going around the Kaaba during the pilgrimage. It starts at the Black Stone, then pilgrims circle the sacred site seven times anticlockwise.

Black Stone
A relic said to be from the time of Adam and Eve. Muhammad set it into the wall of the Kaaba. Pilgrims will kiss, touch or point at it while repeating the takbir, 'God is Greatest'.

The Station of Ibrahim
Metal enclosure containing a stone that features the footprint of the prophet Ibrahim.

Five Pillars of Islam
Acts, mandatory for every Muslim, include: Profession of Faith, Prayer, Almsgiving, Fasting and Hajj (pilgrimage to Mecca).

Pilgrims
In 2017, 2,352,122 people came to Mecca to perform Hajj.

DUBAI

United Arab Emirates
Construction: founded 18th century;
            modern Dubai built from 1960s onwards

A marvel of ambition and planning, Dubai is a gleaming, modern metropolis that defies the hostile desert surrounding it. Dubai was a small trading port with a population of just 20,000 in 1950, but the discovery of oil in 1966 fueled rapid growth. Today it is home to 2.8 million people and is one of the world's fastest-growing economies thanks to booming trade, tourism, aviation, real estate, and financial services. It is also famous for its bold and iconic construction projects, including vast artificial islands and the world's tallest building.

Population
In 2013, 85 per cent of Dubai's residents were foreign-born.

The World
This archipelago of 300 artificial islands forms a map of the world.

The Dubai Mall
The world's second-largest mall by total land area, covering an area equivalent to 50 football pitches. It had 92 million visitors in 2015.

Persian Gulf
The area holds over half the world's oil reserves.

Palm Jumeirah
On completion in 2006, this was the largest artificial island in the world. It has a 520 km (320 mile) long shoreline and a population of 10,500. It is connected to the mainland by a monorail.

4 km
(2.4 miles)

BURJ AL ARAB

BURJ KHALIFA

Palm Jebel Ali
This artificial archipelago was begun in 2002 but has yet to be completed. It was planned to have a population of more than 250,000.

Cost of living
Dubai is currently the most expensive city in the Middle East to live in.

No income tax
A zero-tax policy successfully attracts new investments and workers to Dubai.

Dubai International Airport
The world's busiest airport by international passenger traffic (88,885,367 passengers in 2018).

Sun
In January, the average number of days with precipitation is zero.

New economy
Although the petrochemical industry boosted the development of the city, Dubai actually only has modest oil deposits. Today only 5 per cent of the United Arab Emirates' revenue comes from oil.

BURJ AL ARAB
One of the most beautiful and luxurious hotels in the world.

Super-tall
At 321 m (1,053 ft), Burj Al Arab is the world's 5th-tallest hotel. Dubai also has three more of the top five tallest hotels in the world.

38 per cent of its height is not occupied by any hotel space.

Facilities
Guests can enjoy nine restaurants and bars, five swimming pools, a private beach, wellness club, spa and a turtle rehabilitation centre.

Staff
There are 1,600 members of staff attending to guests' comfort. It has the highest staff-to-suite ratio in the world of 8:1.

Atrium
The 18-storied atrium inside the hotel is 180 m (590 ft) tall.

Suites
Burj Al Arab has 201 suites with areas ranging from 169 m² (1,819 sq ft) to 780 m² (8,396 sq ft). Its most expensive suite starts at $8,900 per night.

Stars
Although it is often called 'the world's only seven-star hotel', it actually has five stars, the maximum rating a hotel can get.

Spacious
The Burj Al Arab is tall, but it only has 28 double-story floors with 202 bedroom suites.

Helipad
210 m (689 ft) above sea level. In 2005, Andre Agassi and Roger Federer played a tennis match here.

Design
Its iconic design made it the first internationally recognisable symbol of Dubai.

Sail
The hotel's shape resembles a billowing spinnaker sail.

Island
The hotel stands on an artificial island built 280 m (919 ft) from the mainland.

Foundations
To build a solid foundation, 230 concrete piles, each 40 m (131 ft) long, were driven into the sand of the island.

It took three years to construct the artificial island, longer than it took to build the hotel itself.

BURJ KHALIFA

Dubai, United Arab Emirates
Construction: 5 years (2004–2009)

With a total height of 829.8 m (2,722 ft), the Burj Khalifa has been the world's tallest building and structure since 2009. Its elegant tapering spire is an iconic symbol of Dubai's ambition and prosperity.

Top dancefloor
The world's highest nightclub is on the 144th floor.

Spire
The spire increases the skyscraper's height by 244 m (800 ft), but adds no usable space.

Spiderman
In 2011, Alain 'Spiderman' Robert climbed the outside of the building all the way to the top in 6 hours.

13-second fall
If you tumbled from the top of the building, your freefall to earth would last 13 seconds.

309,473 m²
The Burj Khalifa's overall floor space is equal to ⅔ the area of the Vatican City.

829.8 m
In 2009, the Burj Khalifa surpassed the world's then-tallest building, Taipei 101 at 439 m (1,440 ft), by a further 320 m – the height of the Chrysler building in New York.

Cost
$ The estimated cost of the project was $1.5 billion.

Elevators
Each of its 57 elevators carry up to 14 people at a speed of 36 km/h (22 mph).

Base

The tower's footprint has three lobes, and was inspired by the *Hymenocallis* flower. This shape gives the structure great stability.

The offset curves of each level of the building were designed to minimise wind resistance.

Less steel

Compared with the Empire State Building, the Burj Khalifa was built using 50 per cent less steel.

Workers

Around 12,000 workers were on site at the peak of the building's construction.

Cleaning

It takes a team of 36 workers four months to clean the building's 24,348 windows.

Water recycling

Condensed water from the air conditioning system is used to irrigate plants in a nearby park.

Water system

100 km (62 miles) of water pipes supply around 946,000 litres (250,000 U.S. gallons) of water, daily. An additional 213 km (132 miles) of pipes are used for the fire emergency system.

Stairs

Climbing Burj Khalifa's 2,909 stairs would take you two hours (if you were feeling fit).

Armani hotel

The skyscraper includes a 304-room hotel created by the famous Italian designer.

Fountain

The building's 270 m (900 ft) long fountain is the second largest choreographed fountain in the world and cost $217 million. It shoots water 150 m (500 ft) into the air.

The Sydney Opera House's cost
of construction increased from
AUS$7 million to AUS$102
million and took 14 years to
complete instead of four.

RABBIT-PROOF & DINGO FENCES

Australia

Construction: 1901–1907 (Rabbit-Proof Fence), 1880–1885 (Dingo Fence)

The longest fences in the world can be found in Australia. The Dingo Fence was built in 1885 to protect sheep flocks in South-Eastern Australia from dingos and other wild dogs. The fence reaches 2 m (6 ft) tall and stretches across 5,614 km (3,488 miles). The Rabbit-Proof Fence was completed in 1907 in a desperate attempt to control the explosive spread of wild rabbits and to protect the crops of Western Australia. It covers 3,256 km (2,021 miles).

Introduction of rabbits

Rabbits were introduced to Australia in 1788 during the first European settlement on the continent. They were bred as food animals under controlled conditions.

Breed like rabbits

In 1859, English settler Thomas Austin released 24 rabbits for hunting purposes. The released rabbits, with virtually no predators, flourished and quickly threatened Australia's ecology and economy.

Effects on ecology

Rabbits' feeding can kill cultivated trees, shrubs and crops and this overgrazing deprives other animals of food and leads to erosion.

RABBIT-PROOF FENCE

This 3,256-km-long (2,023 miles) Western Australian pest-exclusion barrier has three connected fences.

No. 3 Fence

No. 2 Fence

No. 1 Fence

Protecting the west

The Rabbit-Proof Fence was designed to protect agricultural crops in the west of the country against rabbits spreading from the east.

No. 1 Fence

At the time of its completion in 1907, the No. 1 Fence was the longest unbroken fence in the world (1,833 km, 1,139 miles).

Cost

1 km of the fence cost AUS$250 to build.

Perth

The most isolated large city in the world. The nearest neighbouring urban area is 2,130 km (1,324 miles) away.

European rabbit

This species is native to southwestern Europe and northwest Africa. It was also introduced in South America but did not cause such high levels of damage.

Control measures

In 1950, the myxomatosis virus reduced the rabbit population from around 600 million to 100 million. Over time, the animals became resistant and their population was back to 200–300 million by 1991.

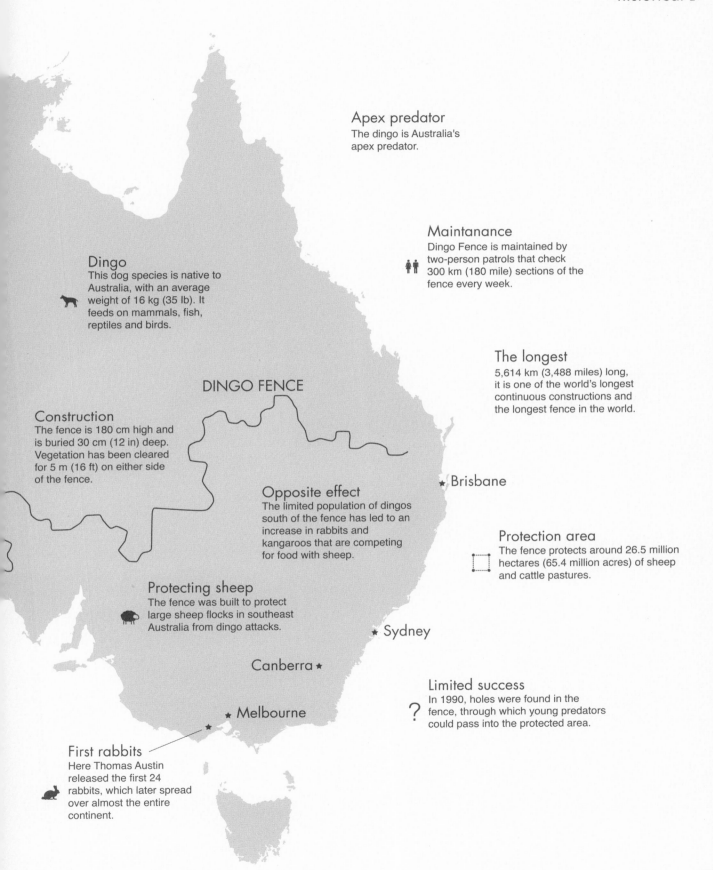

Apex predator
The dingo is Australia's apex predator.

Maintanance
Dingo Fence is maintained by two-person patrols that check 300 km (180 mile) sections of the fence every week.

Dingo
This dog species is native to Australia, with an average weight of 16 kg (35 lb). It feeds on mammals, fish, reptiles and birds.

The longest
5,614 km (3,488 miles) long, it is one of the world's longest continuous constructions and the longest fence in the world.

DINGO FENCE

Construction
The fence is 180 cm high and is buried 30 cm (12 in) deep. Vegetation has been cleared for 5 m (16 ft) on either side of the fence.

Opposite effect
The limited population of dingos south of the fence has led to an increase in rabbits and kangaroos that are competing for food with sheep.

★ Brisbane

Protection area
The fence protects around 26.5 million hectares (65.4 million acres) of sheep and cattle pastures.

Protecting sheep
The fence was built to protect large sheep flocks in southeast Australia from dingo attacks.

★ Sydney

Canberra ★

Limited success
In 1990, holes were found in the fence, through which young predators could pass into the protected area.

★ Melbourne

First rabbits
Here Thomas Austin released the first 24 rabbits, which later spread over almost the entire continent.

SYDNEY OPERA HOUSE

Sydney, Australia
Construction: 14 years (1959–1973)

The Sydney Opera House is one of the most recognisable
structures in the world and a famous symbol of Australia.
It stands on a promontory in Sydney Harbour with its white
sail-like roof structures echoing the maritime heritage of
the area. Its historic location is where some of the first
European settlers on the continent landed.

World Heritage Site
In 2007, the Sydney Opera House
was included on UNESCO's
World Heritage Site list.

Architect
The Danish architect Jørn Utzon beat 232
other projects in the design competition for the
opera house. His prize was 15,000 Australian
pounds in 1957.

He resigned as head designer during
construction after strong criticism from
a politician in the Ministry of Public
Works. He never visited the building.

In 2003, Utzon received the Pritzker
Architecture Prize, one of the world's
premier architecture prizes.

Grand Organ
This instrument is the world's
largest mechanical organ
and has 10,244 pipes.

Concert Hall main shell
The largest of the opera
house's seven venues, this
can host 2,679 spectators.

Design
Designed in the expressionist
style, the building is widely
considered to be one of the
world's most iconic structures.

Underestimation
The cost of the construction
increased from AUS$7 million to
AUS$102 million and took 14
years to complete instead of four.

Spontaneous premiere

In 1960 Paul Robeson became the first
performer at Sydney Opera House
after he climbed the construction and
sang *Ol' Man River* to the workers.

Opening

The opera house was officially opened
in 1973 by Queen Elizabeth II. She
has visited it five times.

Foundations
Construction required 588 concrete
piles to be sunk as deep as 25 m
(82 ft) below sea level.

Visitors
Over 8 million people visit the opera house every year.

Venues
The complex has six indoor venues with a total seating capacity of 5,738.

Events

Around 1,500 events are held in the opera house every year.

I'll not be back
In 1980, Arnold Schwarzenegger won his seventh and final Mr Olympia title here.

Thermoregulation
Orchestras need a temperature of 22.5 °C (72.5 °F) to keep their instruments in tune; 35 km of pipes keep the temperature just right.

Shells
This is the common nickname for the roof structures.

Roof tiles
The roof is covered with 1,056,006 roof tiles, which were shipped from Sweden.

67 m (219 ft)

185 m (607 ft)

Outdoor Forecourt
This open-air venue adds to the six indoor venues.

Sydney Harbour
Inlet of the Tasman Sea. It was here that the British colonists founded a penal colony in 1788, the first mainland settlement in Australia.

Bennelong Point
The building occupies the former Bennelong Island where the house of the Aboriginal cultural interlocutor, Woollarawarre Bennelong, was located.

The International Space Station was built by 16 nations: Belgium, Brazil, Canada, Denmark, France, Germany, Italy, Japan, the Netherlands, Norway, Russia, Spain, Sweden, Switzerland, the UK and the USA.

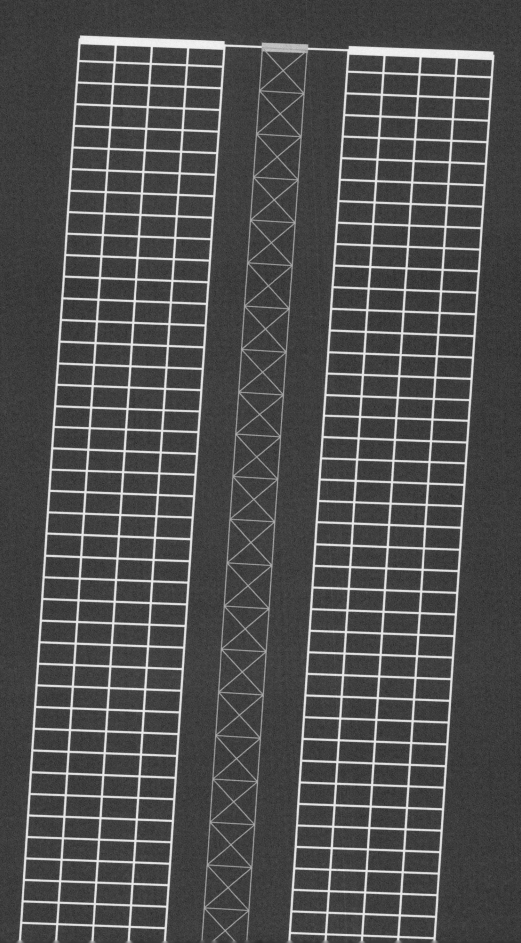

INTERNATIONAL SPACE STATION

Low Earth orbit
Construction: launched in 1998

The International Space Station (ISS) is one of the scientific world's most impressive achievements. The station has been expanded and developed since its initial launch and it has been continuously occupied since its first visitors arrived on 2 November 2000.

The ISS offers a unique environment for scientific research; its crew have performed innovative experiments in biology, physics, astronomy, meteorology and other fields.

Soyuz spacecraft
Used for transporting astronauts to the station, this is currently considered the safest and cheapest means of transport.

Truss radiator panels
Used to disperse heat generated by humans and electronic devices into space.

International project
The station was built jointly by 16 nations: Belgium, Brazil, Canada, Denmark, France, Germany, Italy, Japan, the Netherlands, Norway, Russia, Spain, Sweden, Switzerland, the UK and the US.

Most expensive project
The ISS is the most expensive structure ever built. Its cost was estimated at $150 billion in 2010.

Launch
The first component of the station was launched by Russia in 1998.

Operation timeline
The station is planned to operate until 2030.

Columbus
European science laboratory module.

Orbit
The ISS orbits at an altitude of 330–435 km (205–270 miles) above the planet's surface.

Seen from Earth
The station can be seen from Earth with the naked eye. It's one of the brightest objects in the night sky.

Orbital speed
The station travels at a speed of 27,600 km/h (17,149 mph), which means that it orbits Earth in 92.68 minutes.

Temperature
The temperature in space is -270.45°C (-454.81°F) , which is much lower than the lowest temperature recorded on Earth (-89.2°C (-128.6°F)).

Solar arrays
Generate more than 200 kW of power.

Visitors
The station had been visited by 236 people (as of 14 March 2019) representing 18 nations.

Solar array rotation mount
This keeps the solar arrays pointed towards the Sun.

35 m (115 ft)

Bathrooms
There are two toilets, one built by the Russians and one by the Americans. Urine is filtered back into drinking water.

Training
Astronauts work out for two hours every day to not lose muscle and bone mass due to weightlessness.

Gravity
Technically, at the ISS's altitude, gravity is 90 per cent of that felt on the Earth's surface. However, the effective gravity on the ISS is nearly zero.

Robotic arms
These can be operated remotely from Earth and can be used when the crew are sleeping.

Oxygen
This element essential to life is obtained by electrolysis: water is split into oxygen and hydrogen using energy from the solar panels.

Size
The ISS has around the same volume as a Boeing 747.

Cables
There are over 600 km (373 miles) of cables and wires on the station.

INDEX